If God Were Real

A Journey into a Faith That Matters

John Avant

HOWARD BOOKS
A DIVISION OF SIMON & SCHUSTER
New York   London   Toronto   Sydney

*To my wonderful church, the First Baptist Church
of West Monroe, Louisiana, who has become our family.
Thanks for living like God is real and allowing me
to join you on that journey.*

Our purpose at Howard Books is to:
• *Increase faith* in the hearts of growing Christians
• *Inspire holiness* in the lives of believers
• *Instill hope* in the hearts of struggling people everywhere
Because He's coming again!

Published by Howard Books, a division of Simon & Schuster, Inc.
1230 Avenue of the Americas, New York, NY 10020
www.howardpublishing.com

If God Were Real © 2009 John Avant

ISBN 978-1-4165-8779-8

1 3 5 7 9 10 8 6 4 2

HOWARD and colophon are registered trademarks of Simon & Schuster, Inc.

Manufactured in the United States of America

For information regarding special discounts for bulk purchases,
please contact: Simon & Schuster Special Sales at 1–866–506–1949
or business@simonandschuster.com.

Edited by Between the Lines
Cover design by LUCAS Art & Design, JENISON, MI
Interior design by Davina Mock-Maniscalco

Contents

Acknowledgments

I HAVE THE GREATEST family on this planet. Mom and Dad; Michael and Cindy; my patient and supportive wife, Donna; my gifted and crazy kids, Christi, Amy, and Trey; and Matt and Joseph, the men God has brought into the lives of our daughters—all of you fill my life with joy and motivate me to write. I love you and am proud of each of you. You live as though God is real!

Thanks to all who helped me by giving advice, reading my manuscript, and doing a thousand other things that I could not do without. Thanks to my assistant, Beverly Shoemaker, for keeping me sane through computer problems and for helping with editing.

Thanks to all the prayer warriors and friends who have prayed as I wrote. If God is real, then any good that comes from this book has to be credited to you who actually believe in him enough to pray. I love you all!

Introduction

SHE WAS FOUR years old, the little girl I was going to see on a cold December night. I felt the bite of the Texas wind as I got out of the car in front of a run-down little house. I was dressed in the uniform of our city's police department, where I served as chaplain. In my hands I carried a stuffed animal, a Christmas present for a child I had never met. It seemed almost insulting to think this small gift could mean anything to this little one who had suffered so much.

Our officers had found her at the bottom of a gully—raped, thrown out like trash, and left to die. She was out of the hospital now and staying with her grandmother. As chaplain and as a pastor of a church in the city, I felt I should pay her a visit. But I wondered, as I rang the doorbell, if I would only be making matters worse. How would this victimized little girl react to a strange man coming to see her? Was she so traumatized that she would hide in terror? Would she scream when I entered the house? I knew those were possibilities.

But nothing could have prepared me for her reaction.

Her grandmother answered the door and thanked me for coming as she let me in. Before I could say a word, a precious child who had never seen me before came running across the room and jumped into my arms. She wrapped her tiny arms around my neck and clung to me. Stunned, I simply held her for a long time.

Eventually she let me show her the present I had brought for her. She seemed pleased with it but more interested in me. After a short visit I stood to go, and she leaped into my arms again. She whispered words into my ear that I will never forget: "I wish you were my daddy."

I've thought about that night many times in the years since. Deep inside, at our core, we all want a Father who will hold us. One who will heal us when we're wounded and make things right when they are wrong. A Daddy with big, strong arms.

But is it only a wish, a childish hope no more real than a fairy tale? What if there were no such Father?

I could not be the father that hurting child needed. Only God can be the Father who will love her enough and who is powerful enough to ultimately bring any redeeming good from the hideous evil she'd suffered. If he's really there.

If he's not, the implications for all of life are almost unimaginable.

What If God Is Not Real?

That's the question of all questions, isn't it? The answer affects everything. Who hasn't gazed at the stars on a clear night and, feeling the smallness of our humanity, wondered if we're really all alone in the vastness. If, just maybe, there's nothing out there.

God (if he is real) seems to refuse being "proved." He values faith so much that in his Word (if it really is his), he says that "without faith it is impossible" to please him (Hebrews 11:6).

Yet who among us has not stared at those same stars and felt the awe and majesty of a creation that cries out in proclamation of a Creator—that seems too ridiculously complex to have been an accident?

I believe that God is real. In fact, I believe that the God of the Bible is exactly who he says he is. I believe he has given us enough evidence to believe in him, using intellect as well as faith.

And yet the implications if I were mistaken about God are terrifying, at least for me. It would mean that I am wasting my one shot at life. You see, I have poured my life into serving him, into following this God I love, into the relationship I have with him through his Son, Jesus. I've been in ministry for more than a quarter of a century. I have based my marriage, my parenting, and the very foundation of my life on what I believe about God. If I am wrong, I am wrong about everything that matters.

Evangelistic Atheists

This causes me to take seriously a surprising development in recent years among atheist leaders. It seems to me that some atheists, a few of whom have become bestselling authors, are taking more seriously the possibility that God is *not* real than we Christians are taking the possibility that he *is*! Sam Harris, Richard Dawkins, Daniel Dennett, and Christopher Hitchens are among the most prominent of these atheists. Dawkins calls the group the Four Musketeers. David Aikman, in his book *The Delusion of Disbelief,* has another name for them. He writes: "Harris, Dawkins, Dennett, and Hitchens—the names resonate like stately Anglo-Saxon partners of a Virginia law firm—descended upon the faithful like, well, the Four Horsemen of the Apocalypse."[1]

Atheist leaders seem to understand the ramifications of the existence of God more clearly than most believers. Sam Harris has made quite a stir with his books, *The End of Faith* and *Letter to a Christian Nation.* Take a look at his clear depiction of what is at stake here:

> The Bible is either the word of God, or it isn't. Either Jesus offers humanity the one, true path to salvation (John 14:6), or he does not. We agree that to be a true Christian is to believe that all other faiths are mistaken, and profoundly so. If Christianity is correct, and I persist in my unbelief, I should expect to suffer the torments of hell. Worse still, I have persuaded others, and many close to me, to reject the very idea of God. They too will languish in "eternal fire" (Matthew 25:41). If the basic doctrine of Christianity is correct, I have misused my life in the worst conceivable way. I admit this without a single caveat.[2]

Harris is crystal clear: the question of whether the God of the Bible exists is one of utmost importance. In fact, he, along with a growing group of militant atheists, is willing to commit his life to defeating the idea that God is real. These atheists are evangelistic in their fervor. But I fear that for most Christians, it's just not that big a deal. God has become merely a part of the culture that is taken for granted. He's not really the Lord of all life. He's more like background noise. I get the sense that if he disappeared, we might miss him for a while, like a comfortable jacket we've misplaced, but we wouldn't suffer a substantive loss in our lives. We may believe that he's real . . . we just don't live like he is.

I like atheists. I've known many Christians I'd rather not spend time with, but surprisingly, I can't think of a single atheist I've known whom I didn't like. I have learned from them, respected their honesty, and rejoiced to see some become followers of Christ. I would rather spend time with atheists who know why they don't believe in God than with Christians who don't know why they do. I respect conviction—even if it is the conviction to have no convictions.

Lauren Sandler is one of those atheists I really like. Lauren lives in New York City, and I've had lunch with her a few times, along with my daughter who is an actress there. Lauren's book, *Righteous,* rocked my world. I've quoted from it in sermons more than any other book I've read in recent years. She declares herself an "unrepentant Jewish atheist,"[3] yet she admits that evangelical revival has deeply impacted America in the past and predicts that the next Great Awakening is on the horizon—to be launched by a new generation of radical, young Christ followers. Lauren sees, among young Christians today, "a movement of staggering demographic diversity united by an intensely shared faith." She says, "We are poised before the next Great Awakening in American history."[4]

Quite a prophecy from an atheist! Don't misunderstand her, though. Lauren is far from excited about the coming revival. "I've got news for you: this awakening ain't so great," she writes.[5] In fact, she wrote her book for the express purpose of galvanizing secularists to stop what she sees as a dangerous religious movement in America.

Righteous does have some flaws. Sandler makes the same mistakes of poor exegesis, for instance, as do many atheists writing about the Bible, claiming that Christians believe Levitical law applies today. She also falls back on stereotypes, lumping together people who clearly hold different beliefs, such as Mark Driscoll and Brian McLaren, or claiming that young Christians read nothing except the Bible.

In spite of these flaws, Sandler diagnoses a real sickness in the church today with devastating clarity, while it seems most believers think either the church is in good health or perhaps has just a passing cold. As I read her book, I found myself "Amen-ing" this atheist many times. Listen to Lauren preach: "It's up to us to do what Jesus would do, to reach out to those who believe we are the enemy, to lift up the poor and needy, and to turn the world on its head as he did."[6]

Amen to that! But she adds this twist: "It is time for our own secular Great Awakening."[7] I'm not going to hold my breath waiting for that awakening. "You are an accidental life in an accidental universe and will rot in the ground with no future" does not seem to me capable of providing the energy needed for a national revival movement. I also am not wringing my hands in fear of the new atheists like Sam Harris, and certainly not Lauren Sandler. Atheists are not the enemy. In fact, we can learn from them. If we are disturbed, it should be because they seem to have more passion about what they're convinced doesn't exist than we have about the One who does!

It's time to quit blaming all the typical culprits of evil society for our own failures to be followers of Christ. If what we believe is true, then we already have sufficient power, through Christ, to radically transform our world. But if we continue on our current path, we can't blame the atheists for the pitiful state of the culture. We need only take a long look in the mirror.

So my purpose in writing this book is not to try to defeat the atheists. Nor am I attempting a comprehensive defense of the existence of God. Others can and have done that better than I could.

My purpose here is to confront Christians with a question—

a question that I believe is the single most important question of our lives.

Does it matter if God is real?

What If God Is Real?

Don't answer too quickly. I'm not asking how you feel about this question. I'm asking if it makes any difference in your life. I am asking if, despite all of our loud calls for our rights as Christians in the public square, most of us live like God doesn't really matter that much.

Could it be that we are practical atheists?

Do we think, live, act, and breathe as though the God of the Bible is real? Shouldn't we, if he really lives in us? And if we don't, does that not give atheists a good reason to question whether he's real?

If you've picked up this book and you're an atheist or a seeker of truth, I hope you'll find the considerations in these pages intriguing. After all, there really is no more important question to answer than whether God exists—and if he does, what does that mean for us? So I'll have some challenges for you along the way that I hope will interest you. In fact, I'll make one right now that may shock you.

If you can't find Christians who live like God is real, don't become one.

Shane Claiborne, author of *The Irresistible Revolution*, includes a chapter titled "In Search of a Christian." In it he says, "I knew we were not going to win the masses to Christianity until we began to live it. So I went on a quest. I went looking for a Christian. I looked around hoping to find someone else who might be asking, What if Jesus meant the stuff he said? And I kept coming across dead people."[8]

This is what's scary about my challenge to you who are not believers. With the current state of Christianity, what if all the ones who actually lived like God is real are dead and gone? I would have to say that you have good reason to be suspicious of God's existence if he makes no apparent difference in his followers.

Now, to those of you who believe: how's that for pressure?

But I make no apologies for that statement. This is no game. It's all or nothing. Sam Harris is right: "Either Christ was divine, or he was not. . . . In the fullness of time, one side is really going to win this argument, and the other side is really going to lose."[9]

But I am confident, those of you who don't believe, that the real God will lead you to real Christians. They're out there—I see them every day. And they, in turn, will show you the God who is real.

A lot is at stake here. For me. For you. For those who believe. For those who don't. For those who are still on the journey, somewhere in the middle. So let's consider together what it would mean, how it would change us, what life could be, should be . . . if God were real.

1

If God Were Real ... the Illusions
of Ordinary Life Would Be Shattered

We all need illusions. That's why we love movies.
Monica Bellucci

Shattering the Illusion That Christian Life Is Boring

Who doesn't love a great movie? All of the most exciting and wonderful parts of life are right there on the screen to be enjoyed. Romance? Just come to my house anytime my wife, Donna, is watching television, and there's a pretty good chance she'll be watching *Sleepless in Seattle*. I thought the movie was kind of touching the first time I saw it. But Donna still cries, even now that she has the lines memorized.

As for me, I'll take a movie with raw, masculine courage every time. Nothing beats *Gladiator* or *Braveheart* for making you glad to be a man. Or how about pure adventure, like the Indiana Jones films? What could be more cool than watching Indiana get out of every trap—and along the way eat monkey brains, defeat evil, and get the girl?

Yes, movies are one of life's pleasures—even though we know

that what they show us are just illusions. Could it be that we love movies because they allow us to experience, if only for a little while, what we'll never really have? Or what we aren't sure we can ever really be?

But what if life is meant to exceed even the best of what we see on film?

What if we are meant to live out the greatest romance of all?

What if we are designed to be powerful and courageous?

What if life could actually be filled with suspense and adventure and we really could live happily ever after?

Well, shouldn't we expect all these things to be true if God is real? If the One who created this vast universe with a word really did come and live as one of us, die and rise again for us, and promise to fill us with his Spirit, why would we not expect all that and more? Especially since Jesus himself said he came so that we "may have life, and have it to the full" (John 10:10).

Yes, things don't always go smoothly in the movies. In fact, a movie with no tension is boring. As Christians, we know that we won't live happily ever after until we get to heaven. In this world we will have pain and difficulties—but not boredom! Not if God is real.

The movies that seem so exciting to us might be boring when compared with the real lives we are meant to live.

If we actually lived as though God is real.

My friend Gary Witherall calls this kind of life "adventuring for God." Gary is one of those Christians who really believes in God. He has definitely traded in practical atheism for authentic faith. Gary and his wife, Bonnie, put their authentic faith into action as missionaries in Sidon, Lebanon. Regardless of the personal risk involved in taking their Christian witness to a place where many are hostile to Christianity in general and especially missionaries, Gary and Bonnie sought to show God's truth through their authentic, caring lives. They deeply loved the Palestinian people they served.

The following was written on the website of Operation Mobilization, the mission agency with which Gary and Bonnie served: "Some people talk about being on the cutting edge; some actually live there. Fewer choose to live on the bleeding edge of humanity, where nothing is humanly certain except great need, where risk defies other definitions, where light shines the brighter for the enveloping darkness. Sidon in Lebanon is such a place, and Bonnie and Gary Witherall were some of those few."

Gary's belief has been tested in the most extreme ways. In fact, Gary and Bonnie's life should be made into a movie. It already has been written as a book. *Total Abandon* is the story of Bonnie's murder. Bonnie, a nurse, was shot by a terrorist as she entered the clinic where she cared for Muslim women. The authorities quickly got Gary out of Lebanon. Less than a month after Bonnie's murder, Gary wrote the following in his journal: "Nothing remains and yet I have everything. I lost my wife, my ministry, my beautiful apartment overlooking the Mediterranean, my friends there, my Arabic classes, and three classes a week studying Islam. The little Honda we drove on the bumpy roads through the crazy traffic. The warmth of Bonnie lying quietly asleep next to me. I was robbed but have been found today steadfast, strong as a piece of steel yet completely broken. Lord, sustain me."[1]

Those were not just words in a journal. Since those days of crushing loss, Gary has returned to Lebanon many times, including once with my own daughter. He has stood in front of the place where Bonnie was murdered and preached forgiveness and love to the same culture that killed his wife. And then he sang with my daughter and the others there, . . . "Blessed be the name of the Lord . . . You give and take away . . . My heart will choose to say, . . . 'Lord, blessed be Your name.'"

Those who know Gary watch him live in boldness, forgiveness, joy, and service to others—even to those who would kill what he loved most. Who lives like this? Only those who believe God is real!

That's what it's like to believe in God. Gary is living, breathing, weeping, laughing evidence that God is indeed real. If God does not exist, Gary has done an incredible job of inventing God's impact in his life!

I've gotten to know Gary well since Bonnie's death. I have laughed and cried with him, counseled him, and received counsel from him. And I had the privilege to help officiate his wedding to Helena, his beautiful new wife (and the granddaughter of a martyr).

God is real to Gary. This man believes it—and then actually lives as though he does. This has not led to an easy life, but it has led to the adventure of real life. Gary has known passionate love, tragedy and heartbreak, terror and suspense, renewal and new love, courage, danger, and adventure. All of the things we flock to see in the movies are his in real life.

Living for God shouldn't be boring. When we live as though God is real, the true adventure begins. So maybe, after all, living a boring Christian life is a conscious choice, not an inevitable state. Perhaps for most of us the issue is not whether God is real but whether we really want the life that results from living like he is. Perhaps "adventuring for God" is a little too dangerous and risky for most of us. So the question may be, is it worth it to live as though God is real?

Shattering the Illusions of Religion

I've served as a pastor for twenty-seven years and served in a mission agency for two years. I have had the opportunity to see many lives like Gary's—enough to convince me that only God could be responsible for what I have seen in them. But I have to admit that I've also seen a lot of the opposite—lives of those who believe in God, who love Jesus, but who have just settled into lives that are nothing like the adventure of following the real God. Most of these are not bad people. They love their families and friends, try to live decent lives, and serve in their churches. But something is missing. Many of them are just overwhelmed with the stuff of life. They're too busy trying to figure out how to afford a third car payment or how to get their son's grades up to think much about such "deep" things. They may never have stopped to wonder if there could be something more to their experience of God—something that could dramatically impact those all-consuming daily struggles.

Now, living a life of adventure is not, in itself, evidence that God is real. Some people live lives of reckless adventure without God. But my point is that if God is real, there's no need to live a boring life! We are meant for more. You can live a life of temporary adventure without God, but you cannot be an authentic follower of the real God without adventure. And why would you want to?

Many people do want very much to experience more than what they currently know of God. Every pastor hears regularly from those folks who want to "go deeper." I want a deeper knowledge of God too. In fact, I can't think of anything I want more. But my experience has been that many who want to go deeper are actually afflicted with an insidious spiritual disease I call Deeper-Sleep Syndrome. They make the mistake of thinking that going deeper means getting more knowledge about the Bible, having more Bible studies or worship services, or learning some spiritual mystery that they've somehow missed all these years. But as they dive into these things again and again, they're in danger of going so deep that they end up in a deep spiritual sleep, unconscious of what God really wants. That's Deeper-Sleep Syndrome.

The cure is actually quite simple. If God is real, surely he wants us to know him and to know him deeply. In fact, he says he has already told us all we need to know. "His divine power has given us everything we need for life and godliness through our knowledge of him who called us by his own glory and goodness" (2 Peter 1:3). Knowing more about God is a good thing; but acting on what we know is the real answer. James 2:17 says, "Faith by itself, if it is not accompanied by action, is dead."

So if we were to begin to really live out the teachings of Jesus, we would find ourselves in the middle of an incredible spiritual adventure.

Can it be that simple? After all, isn't that what Christians are already doing? Or at least something close to it?

I'm not so sure. When I examine my own life, I wonder how much I'm really seeking to follow Jesus, to do exactly what he said. Am I just a part of a church system that does its best to reinvent the words of Jesus to make what he said more palatable for our modern sensibilities, more in sync with the ways we really want to live? Maybe the nineteenth-century philosopher Søren Kierkegaard had it right:

> The matter is quite simple. The Bible is very easy to understand. But we Christians are a bunch of scheming swindlers. We pretend to be unable to understand it because we know very well that the minute we understand we are obliged to act accordingly. . . . My God, you will say, if I do that my whole life will be ruined. How would I get on in the world?
>
> Herein lies the real place of Christian scholarship. Christian scholarship is the Church's prodigious invention to defend itself against the Bible, to ensure that we can continue to be good Christians without the Bible coming too close. Oh, priceless scholarship, what would we do without you? Dreadful it is to fall into the hands of the living God. Yes, it is even dreadful to be alone with the New Testament.[2]

Wow. I don't think I would be quite that hard on scholarship, but he has a point. If God is real, he has told us what we need to know and what we need to do. Could it be that it's time to take what we know . . . and do it?

I think we need to be prepared for the ramifications of this. We could be talking about a complete reshaping of how we have "done" our faith. But wouldn't that be worthwhile if it resulted in the kind of movement that changed the world, the very course of history, through a little group of peasant nobodies in the first century?

So where do we start? First of all, start with hope—wild, fantastic hope that your life could be worthy of the big screen. That all that captivates us while we sit with our popcorn and Cokes may not be just an illusion.

It is time to be "dis-illusioned."

I stumbled upon a website that fascinates me. It's called "The Joy of Disillusionment: A Resource for Those Leaving Christianity,"[3] and it chronicles the journey and the thoughts of David P. Crews, who has moved from being a committed Christian, a self-professed believer in the God of the Bible, to being an atheist. Crews says, "This site is primarily directed to a select group of people—those who are somewhere in the process of leaving their Christian beliefs behind them and moving forward into an unknown realm of rational, non-theistic thought and life."[4] In other words, he writes to those who once lived as though God is real but now are on a journey to live as though he is not. I found that ironic and intriguing, since I'm writing to people who may not live as though God is real but are on a journey to live as though he is.

I find Crews' writings to be honest and fair and even instructive in a strange, backward kind of way. He writes: "For those of us who have come out of a religious life to the acceptance of disbelief and of a rational world view, the word *disillusionment* is uniquely appropriate, but in a new and positive way. In fact, it is the perfect term for us. When we dissect this word, the root is, of course, 'illusion.' To be 'dis-illusioned,' therefore, is to not be deceived by the illusion. Finally, it is to reject the illusion in favor of what is real."[5]

Strangely enough, I find this to be a great description of how Christ followers need to live if we believe God is real. We must come out of the current religious life we've been languishing in. We must "disbelieve" it. It is not a rational worldview to live in bland uniformity and creative vacuity if we believe what we say we believe. It is time to leave behind that illusion—to reject it in favor of what is real, the God on whom we have staked everything.

Crews goes on to give us a good prescription for living the "disillusioned" life. "When we replace illusion with reality, we step out of our cavern of myth and take a deep breath of the air outside—brisk and with a tang of scents unknown. It is the real world we are inhaling and it enlivens us to move forward and to value who and what we truly are."[6]

Yes! This atheist has just about nailed what life as a Christ follower ought to be.

But I don't know what I find sadder, the fact that David Crews has concluded that God is an illusion or the fact that we so often and so tragically live as though he is. It is time for us to step out of our cavern of myth—in which we live as though we were godless—and breathe the air God made in the same awesome, exhilarating way he made us to breathe it. Or else get honest and follow Crews into a life of less hypocrisy that simply discounts God altogether.

If you're ready to be "disillusioned"—if you are determined to live a life that is genuine, a life that embraces the reality of God rather than the illusion we seem to have made him—I affirm your path. I respect David Crews. In fact, I suspect I would like him. But I believe he is wrong, and desperately so. Our hope is valid. It's intellectually defensible. It's philosophically sound. But it's rarely lived.

So let's begin to live! All the romance and adventure of the most thrilling movies may actually be your birthright as a child of God. The curtain could be lifting, and the screenplay of your life could be about to come alive in a way that would make every flick you've ever seen a B film that can't even begin to measure up.

Shattering the Illusion That Hollywood Must Be Our Enemy

If we truly lived adventurous lives that reflect the reality of God, maybe Christ followers would make all the movies. No, I'm not talking about some battle plan to boycott Hollywood until the purveyors of on-screen smut go broke and Christians take over. (The fact that some have tried things like this fits the sad caricature of Christians the world thinks is true of all of us.) I'm saying that if we made movies that resembled the lives we are actually meant to live, the movies would be so good that everyone would want to see them!

All right, I know I'm being naive. We would leave out the sexual content that draws many people, and not everyone would flock to see our films. But the fact is that many of the best movies actually are about spiritual truths. It almost seems that the world is trying to write our stories for us. I am astounded at the prevalence of spiritual searching evident in movies today. Sometimes the world seems more interested in the wonders and possibilities of God than his followers are.

Tom Hanks seems to bring elements of the gospel into just about every film he stars in. He's the one who lays down his life for another in *Saving Private Ryan*. He's the simple man, Forrest Gump, who just can't get away from the amazing plan and purpose woven throughout his life. Gump is a simpleton, yet he confronts the atheist with a profoundly faith-filled statement: "I'm going to heaven, Lieutenant Dan." And then he witnesses Dan's transformation. Hanks is the lost man in *Cast Away* who experiences the worst we might imagine life could offer and, in the end, sees that there's a plan by which all things work together for his good.

You just can't get away from God and his mysteries in the movies. And even when it's not blatant or intentional, many films seem almost like a retelling of the gospel.

I recently saw the blockbuster movie *I Am Legend*, starring Will Smith. When the film ended, I walked out of the theater thinking, *Well, they did it again! They just made a film that directly parallels the gospel, and they probably had no idea!* (Spoiler alert! If you haven't seen the movie and don't want to know the ending, you might want to skip ahead to the next paragraph—or better yet, go see it and then keep reading.) A man-made virus has virtually destroyed humanity. Those not killed by the disease have been devoured by the horrific creatures that those infected by the virus became. Will Smith's character is a doctor, the only survivor in New York City. He spends his days seeking a cure that will transform the monsters mankind has become back into what they were created to be. At the end he sacrifices his life to save others and, ultimately, the entire world. And what is the means of this salvation? Blood.

Hello? Does anyone have any trouble seeing the gospel reflected in this story? A savior comes and sheds his blood to save and transform the human race, which has been infected by sin. It seems that God's plan is so hardwired into our souls that it leaks out everywhere, even when it may not be intentional.

Does it not seem strange and sad to you, though, that many people who claim to be Christians spend most of their time focusing on the internal issues of church life that almost no one outside of the church cares about, i.e., the style of music and minor doctrinal disputes, while the world scrambles to write our story? And when the creative work of a follower of Christ actually does make the screen, most of the time the world flocks to see it! Films based on J. R. R. Tolkien's The Lord of the Rings trilogy and C. S. Lewis's The Chronicles of Narnia are perfect examples.

The bottom line is, followers of Christ have a compelling story to tell. In fact, if we live like God is real, we have the story of all stories to tell! And we are made to tell it. The foundation of all our stories is that we were made in the image of God—in the image of the Creator. So we were designed to create. The spark that lit the match of the universe ignites our souls.

Yet we seem to think that being a good Christian means pouring water on that spark so it doesn't flame up and get too wild. After all, we have to be reverent, don't we?

What does that even mean? I've heard the "irreverent" criticism used hundreds of times to justify the squelching of creativity within the church. The critics don't always use the words *reverent* or *irreverent*. They may just criticize the music for being too loud or worldly, or the methods of the church too contemporary. But it all seems to come back to the same thing: they want their Christianity to be neatly packaged, safe and quiet—reverent.

My problem is that Jesus' behavior as recorded in the Bible doesn't seem all that reverent to me. He condemned the teachers of the law and Pharisees—the most reverent of Jews—called them names like snakes and vipers, and chose to spend most of his time among big, loud crowds of peasants. He chose rough fishermen and embezzling tax collectors for his followers. He ran those in the religious business out of the temple with a whip.

Jesus calls us to passion, not boredom. Maybe it is time to reject cold "reverence" and join a "wild" crowd. And tell a "wild" story.

My "wild" daughter is a theater actress in New York City. Maybe she can help us understand the story we are meant to tell; the real-life adventure we are meant to live; what the screenplay can look like when we choose to follow Jesus with passion in the real world.

Acting Out God's Love
Christi Avant Watson

Rehearsal studios in Manhattan commonly smell of sweat and bare feet—not an altogether appealing aroma, but one I am familiar with nonetheless. Actors file into this pungent building, chatting excitedly. We are in the ensemble of a play going up at a rather prestigious off-Broadway theater. None of us has any lines. We sing only one song in the show. Nevertheless, we are buzzing like honey-starved bees, knowing that after this production, we can place the name of this theater prominently on our résumés. We hope the next casting director we see will observe this credit, jump for joy, and call us in for every project he has. Most likely, this will not happen; but we hope. After all, we are a people of crazy hope, illogical dreams, and gritty passion. An average person may go to five or six job interviews in a lifetime; we go to five or six a week. If one produces any results, even a follow-up phone call, we celebrate.

Halfway through rehearsal, a presence enters the room, and all eyes turn in her direction. Dressed head to toe in the quintessential New York hue—black—the acclaimed playwright has joined the lowly ensemble players. In the middle of the room, she stands on a chair and warmly greets us. "I grew up in a strict evangelical home," she says, "then I went to Berkeley, and I began to accept what is so acceptable today—that evangelicals are morons, idiots, and that they are ruining our world. However, after I moved to New York, I began to realize that to lump all of these people together is a bit simple-minded. I decided to do an experiment, to write the church service—and the characters in that service—that would interest me as an atheist; and that is the history behind the show you are in." If I was buzzing before, now I was spinning out of control with anticipation. The only thing I love as much as singing or delving into an intriguing character is working with and knowing artists who are aggressively, and in this case publicly, searching for truth. Creative people, whether or not they follow Christ, have tapped into the remnants of God left in every human heart, and I absolutely love surrounding myself with that.

For two years I have been here, pursuing this absurd profession alongside New York's progressive and wonderful culture. I have had the privilege of performing all over the United States, even in Alaska. Every day is not a good day. Some days I feel like I have been thrown into a boxing ring, gloveless and in five-inch heels, and been pitted against a heavyweight champion. On those days I focus on the relationships I have developed that would never have taken root within the walls of a church. Although my friends are very spiritual, they tend to fall somewhere along the playwright's path. Either they have been wounded and are angry or they simply feel that the Christian church is irrelevant.

Often the church has not helped matters. Sometimes the church sings "Just As I Am" and then demands that others be just as she is.

Every day I pray that I can be a part of reversing the tragic flow that has left the state of the Christian church such that this is its impression on the world—or at least that I can follow Jesus Christ closely enough to heal the pain people feel.

Eric Bryant, one of the pastors at a "flow-reversing" church in Los Angeles, says that "Love is the best apologetic." After all, was it not love that drove Jesus Christ to hell and back on our behalf? No other force is powerful enough to turn the tide, and as ambassadors of that love, we have an amazing opportunity to alter the future.

Perhaps I'll never grace a Broadway stage or a big screen. Perhaps I'll never again get paid to do what I know I was born to. These thoughts are paralyzing sometimes, but all adventures come with great risk. In the end, the faces of my friends who have allowed me to share in their spiritual journeys are what matters. It is not the grandiose feats you accomplish but the people you actively and intentionally love who will take you on the great adventure available to every follower of Christ. If you restrict your love to those like you, those you understand, those who make you feel comfortable, you will be pretty bored. If you dare to open your life to one person who needs a friend, you just might find yourself in an adventure of eternal proportions.

Since we have the most compelling and interesting story to tell, and since it seems even those who don't believe our story want to tell it for us, maybe it's time that we actually begin to tell it ourselves—and even more important, to live it ourselves. To live like God is real.

The screenplays of the movies of our lives will be full of emotional ups and downs, joy and sorrow, laughter and tears. Like Gary and Bonnie Witherall's missionary service in Lebanon, like my daughter Christi's missionary service in the theater district of New York, authentic life in Christ will not always be easy, pleasant, or predictable.

But it will always be an adventure.

Trading Illusions for a Compelling Faith

I walked past the television the other day and stopped in my tracks when I heard a voice say, "I have been told you will not have a person of faith at your house. . . . Is that true?" The voice belonged to talk-show host Glenn Beck, and his question was addressed to comedian and illusionist Penn Jillette, who is well known for his controversial atheistic ideas. Jillette confirmed that Beck was correct and went on to explain why he would not allow Christians or other people of faith to visit in his home. He said that he did not use alcohol or drugs and would not allow people who did into his home to influence his children. He also did not want what he had seen in Christianity to influence his children in any way.[7]

Is it possible that while we Christians have been busy fighting the culture war and protecting our families from evil influences, we have done such a poor job of living out an intelligent, provocative, and compelling faith that people like Jillette now feel they must protect their children from us? After almost thirty years of ministry, I'm not sure he has it wrong. I've been fortunate to spend my ministry among loving people who helped my children to grow up seeing much of the good that is the church. But honestly, I've seen more children alienated from God and from the church by the actions of Christians than by anything atheists have done. I've lost count of the number of pastors I know whose children want nothing to do with the God of their parents, because they watched what people who claimed to love God did to those parents. Even I want to protect my children from some Christians.

In a different interview, with NPR, Jillette said, "Believing there is no God gives me more room for belief in family, people, love, truth, beauty, sex, Jell-O, and all other things I can prove and that make this life the best life I will ever have."[8] Now *that's* funny. And also profoundly sad. For I believe the responsibility lies squarely at the feet of the church for allowing an illusionist like Penn Jillette to spend his whole life seeing only an illusion of what it means to follow Jesus, never the real thing. For offering so little of Jesus to the world that a man like Jillette can really think that all those things he mentioned, from his family to his Jell-O, are better off without God, without purpose, without hope of anything except utter annihilation, and without any contact from Christians. It's time that we change that, for Jillette's sake and for millions of others'. It's time to become the kind of people everyone wants to have over to his house—if nothing else, just to hear our stories, to explore the mystery of our lives, to try to understand what it is about us that draws them to us, even in their disbelief. It's time to get the messed-up movie we've made of Christianity out of the theater and put a new show on the screen.

One that is worthy of the Producer.

So take a step toward that hope's becoming reality. Decide to take the risk of living like God is real, whatever that may mean and wherever that may take you. Perhaps the only way you'll be sure that God is real is to live as if he is and then watch what happens. Get ready, though. In the next chapter we'll see just how enormous that change may be.

2

If God Were Real . . .
We'd All Give Up on Christianity

Christianity seems like an old, broken-down building
that I have to drive by every day.
I don't even notice it any more.
Eric, twenty-nine years old, quoted in *UnChristian*

AFTER MORE THAN thirty years of following Jesus, I've given up on "Christianity" as most of us know it. I think I gave up some time ago, but it has taken me a little while to admit it. I owe a lot of the good things in my life to the structures and institutions of Christianity. I've contributed a lot of the years of my life to its advancement. I've stood behind pulpits and boldly proclaimed the message of the Religious Right. I registered voters, passed out voter guides, marched in an occasional protest, and even helped lead a few boycotts—two of which made the news. I joined the battle of the righteous against the evil, Christianity against the rest of the nasty world. I was a frontline soldier. I staked my life and gave my all for the advancement of Christianity.

I was wrong.

In spite of all the time and effort I devoted for all those years,

I have abandoned my commitment to "Christianity." In this I have joined the atheists.

I want to be very clear about what I am rejecting. I am giving up on Christianity as a religion, as an institution, and as the system that it has largely become. This kind of Christianity is a fraud and a failure—because this is never what the Christian movement was meant to be!

Jesus did not come to start a "Christian religion." He did not come to establish "Christendom." And he sure didn't come to institute "the Christian religious system." Those things, in many ways, are the antithesis of what he came to do. They represent more closely those who wanted him dead! Sure, every movement will have organizations, guidelines, and structures. But when the organization *becomes* those things, it has failed. So Christianity as we have made it is a fraud and a failure. No one needs it anymore, if one ever did.

In the first-century church, the word *Christianity* described something much closer to a Jesus Movement than to the mess we call Christianity today.

Even the best apologetic I've ever read, *The Faith,* by Charles Colson and Harold Fickett, is not really a defense of Christianity. Colson says:

> On a number of occasions I have stopped in the middle of giving talks and asked, "What is Christianity anyway?"
> . . . Christians must see that the faith is more than a religion or even a relationship with Jesus; *the faith is a complete view of the world and humankind's place in it.* Christianity is a worldview that speaks to every area of life.[1]

Colson is defending our faith, not institutional Christianity. We need faith. "Christianity"? Not so much. I know these are strong words. So allow me to present my case.

Five reasons why I've given up on Christianity— and why you should too

Reason 1: Christianity Crucifies Christians

I thoroughly enjoyed the book *I Sold My Soul on eBay* by Hemant Mehta—the "friendly atheist," as he calls himself. Mehta does seem friendly to me, and I think I'd like him. He says, "I am not angry with God and I don't want to rid the world of religion. . . . I hope you will think of me not simply as an atheist, but rather as a person with questions about faith, an openness to evidence that might contradict my current beliefs, and a curiosity about Christianity and its message."[2]

Though Mehta does not believe in the soul, he put his up for auction. Actually, he simply allowed the highest bidder to send him to church. The winning bidder had Mehta travel to many churches and write a review of his experiences. As I read each review, I realized that this atheist was criticizing many of the same things that had been bothering me for years.

I was reading this book on vacation, and sitting by the pool one day, I shocked Donna by saying, "I think I want to be an atheist." She hit me on the arm. Now, I'm not an atheist. I'm not really tempted to become an atheist. But I found myself wanting to be free to think like an atheist. An atheist can look at what we do in our churches and say, "That's ridiculous," or "Why would anyone who believes in God act this way?" or "Doesn't much of this fly right in the face of what the Bible actually teaches?" But as a representative of Christianity, as a member of the club, it's dangerous to say these things, to ask too many questions. You could lose the respect of your peers. You might lose your position, your livelihood, your friends. You could lose your membership in the club. And believe me, no group of people in this world knows how to tear people apart like Christians.

Reggie McNeal understands this. He wrote a great book called *The Present Future: Six Tough Questions for the Church.* As I read it, I felt as though I'd found a kindred spirit. He points out that when you begin to question anything about the state of Christianity today, many people will label you a heretic. "It is easier for some people," McNeal says, "to relegate me to heresy than to deal with the issues I raise. I am particularly nervous about this charge. I know what the church has done to heretics. It's not dying that's scary. It's what they do to you before they let you die that frightens me."[3]

I'm with you, Reggie. You want to be as careful about offending or saying the "forbidden things" around some Christians as you would about slapping the Godfather's mama. Go online and do a little research for yourself. Read the crazy things Christians write about one another. Heresy hunters are everywhere. Personal attacks abound. Gossip is rampant. Reputations are destroyed. Church members create websites to attack their pastors. Blogs have become big-time online gossip sites where the rules from Scripture we claim to believe don't seem to apply. We can slander away with no shame as long as we can hide behind our screen names of sounddoctrine777 or truthmonitor888.

And politics? We're the masters. After all, evangelicals have been largely responsible for turning the tide of so many elections. Why not bring those same tactics into the realm of Christianity?

Experts in political maneuvering abound. I know. I've been in the meetings. I've seen the raw power grabs. I've sometimes allowed my own ego to go there too. But there's always been something in my spirit that has bothered me about all this. I thought we believed in someone called the Holy Spirit—someone who could work in the hearts of people; bring change to lives, cultures, cities, and nations; someone we could trust to move among us, to lead us and guide us without all our petty maneuvering. Someone who is real. How does this mesh with all of the conniving and plotting I see so much in Christianity? I find little evidence to convince me that the God we say we believe in is the God of this "Christianity."

Jesus could hardly have been clearer about how we are to respond to one another as his followers: "A new command I give you: Love one another. As I have loved you, so you must love one another. By this all men will know that you are my disciples, if you love one another" (John 13:34–35). We are to love one another in the same way Jesus loves us! That's big. That's not humanly possible. That's why God has to be real for it to actually happen. And when it does happen, it's one of the great evidences for the world to see that he is real: "By this all men will know that you are my disciples" (John 13:35).

I have watched this kind of love for almost three decades of ministry. I've seen it in ways that have strengthened my faith and deepened my love for the God whom I believe is the source of all love. I have seen it in quiet ways—in the selfless ways Christians care for one another when they suffer sickness, death, tragedy, and sorrow. And I have also seen it in supernatural ways that transcend human understanding.

I have a friend in the Middle East. I've written about him in my book *Authentic Power.* I didn't use his real name in order to protect him, but he tells his own story so publicly now that there's little protection in secrecy. His name is Samer. Samer was a radical Islamic extremist who had memorized half the Koran and regularly gave the call to prayer at the most radical mosque in his city. His heart was ruled by hatred. He trained and prepared to kill infidels. When I first met him, he told me that if he had met me three years earlier, he would have killed me! He followed that rather unsettling comment with a bear hug of an embrace and a joyful laugh that I have come to know well.

My friend Samer is a follower of Christ now and an evangelist in the Middle East. His conversion was a miracle, but that's a story for another time. The resulting change in him, the raging hatred transformed into selfless love—that is a story for now.

Samer's own family kidnapped him after his conversion and have since sought to kill him. Yet he has loved them and cared for them in such a way that they've begun to change. He has risked his life to provide for them and share the gospel with them in the Palestinian refugee camp where they live. And as a result, Samer's mother came to Christ just before she died.

Samer has become a dear friend. I have come to love and trust this man who once wanted to kill people like me and my family. In fact I sent my own eighteen-year-old daughter to live in Lebanon for a summer and to learn from him.

Recently Samer met a group of Jewish followers of Christ. He told them his story—and that there was no group of people in the world he had hated more than Jews. Then he told them of his change, of what Jesus had done in him, and of the deep love God had placed in his heart for those he'd once hated. And then he did something amazing.

He washed their feet.

And then they washed his. I have the pictures of this. Such a transformation is not normal. It's beyond human. It's the love of Jesus in action, and it's one of the many examples of why I believe in him.

The problem is that this kind of Christ-like love is meant to be the normal life of a Christ follower. But as so many Christians languish in institutional, religious "Christianity," the transforming love of Christ is increasingly driven out, replaced by our own love for power, control, position, and prestige. Not too many feet are being washed these days.

I have pointed these things out to those who would listen for several years now. I specifically asked one of the most prominent leaders in Christianity how we can act the way we do toward one another in such clear contradiction to the Scriptures we say we believe. He smiled and complimented me on how idealistic I am. He explained that sometimes it's impossible to live out the specific biblical teachings about love in the real world and reminded me of what he had told me several times before: that I was a little naive . . . but that it was refreshing.

I've thought about that conversation many times in my journey away from institutionalized Christianity. The good news is that I've been cured of both my idealism and my naïveté. I now find myself fully and painfully aware of the empty shell that the institution of Christianity has become.

Reason 2: Christianity Demonizes Those God Loves

When Mehta visited those many churches, he encountered the same surprise over and over. He said, "I kept running across a consistent and troubling truth about American Christianity. It is clear that most churches have aligned themselves against nonreligious people. By adopting this stance, Christians have turned off the people I would think they want to connect with."[4]

How crazy is this? That we would turn the Great Commission into the Great Opposition!

In my days at a missions agency, traveling every week to many churches across the country, I saw it over and over. Most Christians are either so sheltered within the religious shell of their churches that they don't really know any non-Christians, or they are actively working to oppose them. Or both. This is pretty bizarre considering the fact that the only people we have a record of Jesus opposing were religious leaders. The worst of the worst of his day were drawn to him, not repelled by him. Jesus consistently sought them out, had dinner with them, talked with them, and went to their parties. As far as I can discover, he never boycotted them, rallied against them, or declared them the reason for all the world's woes. He just loved them.

It seems to me that the modern system of Christianity pushes us to do what advances the system, what's best for the religion. Jesus calls us to what's best for each person he lived and died for.

My friend Lauren Sandler writes about what happened to a young youth minister she met named Ted Bruun. Ted was serving in a church in Twin Falls, Idaho. He did a fantastic job of following the example of Jesus. Ted went to the gangs and other marginalized students in the area and invited them to parties at the church. God began to move in phenomenal ways. Attendance doubled each week. The entire youth culture of Twin Falls began to change. But listen to Lauren's account of what happened next: "Church members despised him for bringing these kids into their midst. During one service, Ted reported to the congregation about a major success the night before, the sort of achievement youth workers dream of: a mass of kids had flushed their entire drug stash down the toilets in the church bathroom. Instead of applauding, a parishioner shouted, 'Do you know what that can do to our plumbing?' and walked out, a line of grumbling dissenters forming behind him."[5]

Unfortunately this is not an aberration. This is "Christianity" in its normal, deadly manifestation these days. It's the reason I am done with it. After that event, by the way, so was Ted. Sandler reports that half the church left over that episode, and "Ted began to feel that church mentality was no different than gang mentality—an exclusive group with a dress code and a set of rules to live by, where no deviation from the institution would be tolerated. And so several years ago Ted left the church, too."[6]

If I am to follow Jesus, I can't follow that kind of Christianity anymore. It no longer seems to have much to do with him.

Reason 3: Christianity Doesn't Take God Seriously

If God is real, he is the most significant factor in our lives and our future, and he must be taken seriously! He must affect the way we live—everything about the way we live. But I see little evidence of that in contemporary Christianity.

Shane Claiborne takes God seriously. He has wondered aloud for years what would happen if a church actually took seriously the things the Bible says. Now he's leading a church to actually try it. He's one of the founding members of the Simple Way, a community seeking to follow Christ, in Philadelphia. He writes about this in *Irresistible Revolution*. It seems to be a pretty incredible group. The Simple Way simply seeks to follow Jesus—to love him, to love one another, and to truly love its community, especially "the least of these."

When I read about what Shane is doing, I feel alive with hope. So much of it sounds like a movement I read about in the book of Acts. Now, I admit that some of Claiborne's beliefs are controversial. I vacillate between excitement over the way they're living and discomfort with some of the theological broadness and perhaps a naive acceptance of some liberal political views.

But at least Shane is trying to take God seriously. The Bible also says, "Watch your life and doctrine closely. Persevere in them, because if you do, you will save both yourself and your hearers" (1 Timothy 4:16). Shane appears to have the "life" part down pretty well, at least. And honestly, I've begun to wonder which is more important. Now, this is hard for a guy like me—a committed biblical conservative—to say; but which do you think Jesus would be more concerned about in our lives, doctrine or action? In all his dealings with the Pharisees, does it not look like he was almost dismissive of their doctrine when their lives looked like "whitewashed tombs" (Matthew 23:27)? I think I would like to avoid having Jesus call me a "snake." And if possible, I'd like to have him call the church I pastor something other than "a brood of vipers" (Matthew 23:33).

It seems to me that the Bible calls for balance. Doctrine matters. But are we meant to spend all of our time fighting over it when far too many studies suggest that our actions are no different from the actions of those who don't believe in God? I have to wonder: if we began acting like Jesus, wouldn't it be a whole lot easier to believe like Jesus?

My friend Ed Stetzer is a great researcher, is committed to the God of the Bible, and believes every word of it. But what I most like about him is that he's not afraid to speak out when we, as Christians, mess things up. I asked him for some solid evidence: Do Christians generally live as though God is real? Do our lives look measurably different from those who don't believe he is? Here's Ed's response.

Sleeping Awake
ED STETZER

This year I've talked to more than forty thousand pastors and church leaders. A lot of them love Jesus. A lot of them are trying to make an impact. Some are skinny, some fat, some pretty, and some ugly. But I have not just talked . . . I have listened. From their stories, thousands of them, I have learned much about Christians in America.

I can tell you that there are many reasons (shining examples, actually) to think the church is alive and kicking; yet, where it really counts, it's sound asleep. I have heard the stories many times and have lots of anecdotal evidence pointing to a sleeping church. But now there's proof.

LifeWay Research has produced results from a groundbreaking survey that included 2,500 adults who attend a Protestant church in America at least once a month or more. It reveals some alarming facts.

To begin with, Christians live as though God is not real.

When they realize that some aspect of their life is not right in God's eyes, only 23 percent make necessary changes.

Stop and let that sink in. Less than a quarter of believers actually make changes based on their relationship with God.

While the church has spent years trying to convince itself that it's awake, it's actually tightly snuggled under the covers. Now we're threatened with this sobering reality: that the majority of us aren't "us." The "church" is now one of the greatest mission fields, filled with people who say they know God but don't live like they follow him.

Even more alarming:

- Only 36 percent of these churchgoers strongly agree that they honestly put God first in their lives, even with reference to their values and priorities.
- Just 54 percent of churchgoers strongly agree that they desire to please and honor Jesus in all that they do.
- A mere 37 percent strongly agree that they have made a serious attempt to discover God's will for their lives.
- And only 28 percent of all respondents strongly believed that a Christian must learn to deny himself or herself in order to serve Christ.

This research exposes a discipleship weakness and an insular church. While people attend services, the message isn't sticking. The most disheartening fact of all: many people have figured out how to live without God and still claim him.

The weakness in discipleship and theology tells us that we haven't been spending our time, resources, and messages on the right thing. When you have these kinds of views of the

Christian faith, you get gospel-lite. The apostle Paul wrote to the Roman church, but his words speak just as pointedly to the American church more than two thousand years later: "It is already the hour for you to wake up from sleep, for now our salvation is nearer than when we first believed. The night is nearly over, and the daylight is near, so let us discard the deeds of darkness and put on the armor of light" (Romans 13:11–12 HCSB).

Our downward spiral tells us that it's time to re-soil. We have more resources than ever. People learn to raise their kids from James Dobson. Dave Ramsey teaches us how to handle our money. John Maxwell teaches us how to lead. We have spiritual meccas all over the place (I work for one), and we're still not getting it done.

The evangelical bubble is a failure.

Obviously, it's complicated. And we cannot boil it down to one solution. But we do have a big problem on our hands: we now have a church that doesn't truly believe anymore.

The question we need to be asking is this: how can we raise up robust disciples? That must be the heartbeat of our mission.

The fact is, when Christians do not put a high priority on Jesus' teachings, one has to ask why. And what are we to do?

Well, I can tell you this: In the first seconds of waking up in the morning, there's a slight squint to my eyes. It's not the most comfortable place to be, and I'd rather go back to sleep. But my mind tells me that if I don't keep going, there will be consequences. So I down a cup of coffee, hop in the shower, and jump into the day.

And that's exactly what the church needs to do about the

disciplines involved in making disciples. No one said it's going to be easy to change.

We need to not confuse believers as to how to live the Christian life. Giving them a half-gospel message is wrong; they deserve better. We've tried it, and it doesn't produce disciples.

Søren Kierkegaard once told a parable about ducks going to church. They listened to a duck preacher explain how God had given them wings to fly—and they could go anywhere with those wings. They would do what God told them to with those wings. They could fly into the presence of God.

They all shouted amen . . . and then waddled home.

The greatest threat is not that the church is sleeping but that it thinks it's awake. It thinks that this waddling is all that God has for it.

Let's not waddle. Let's grab a cup of coffee, hop in the shower, and wake up the church!

It's time for the church to take flight and be who we are meant to be. Otherwise we don't have a good answer for the atheists who live like there is no God . . . because we do too!

Atheists like Dawkins, Harris, and Hitchens are different from Sandler and Mehta. They don't see themselves as friendly toward Christians. They're more likely to share the attitude of Penn Gillette and not want us in their homes—or in existence for that matter. They write whole books (or at least chapters of books) about how little difference Christianity makes in the way we live. And sometimes they tell the truth—that some forms of Christianity can be a destructive force in our world. After all, there have been times before now when Christians didn't take God seriously. Slavery comes to mind.

It's not a pleasant thing for me to agree with these hostile atheists that Christianity needs to be eliminated. But before militant atheists mount more attacks against a Christian system that appears to be dying anyway, maybe the better answer is the suicide of our system. I don't care if I see formal Christianity anymore. I just want to see Christians!

And they're out there everywhere, as I've already said. Real, live, Jesus-following, difference-making servants of a real God. But the Christian system either hides them in its dark shadows or opposes them directly.

Shane Claiborne writes: "If you ask most people what Christians believe, they can tell you, 'Christians believe that Jesus is God's Son and that Jesus rose from the dead.' But if you ask the average person how Christians live, they are struck silent. We have not shown the world another way of doing life. Christians pretty much live like everybody else; they just sprinkle a little Jesus in along the way."[7]

Yeah.

That's what's driving me out of "Christianity." And yet I recognize that I'm part of the problem. I've found that the longer I hang around in the world of "Christianity," the more my own sprinkler system is activated. I'm drawn away from the hard stuff of really following Jesus to the sweet rewards of staying tight within the system and defending the status quo. I don't like myself as a Jesus sprinkler. I'm going after another way.

I love Christ.

I love Christians.

Okay, I probably don't love all of them, but I love many of them.

My point is that my problem is not with Jesus or with his followers. I just don't want to waste this one life I have on a system that doesn't take God seriously. Christians have always fallen short. We love Jesus, but we are not him. We often fail to live like he is real. But what gets me is that the system called Christianity seems to be okay with all this. As long as the right people are elected, the right sins opposed, the right people in control, the right church structures maintained, and the right stuff believed, it doesn't seem to really matter if we make any difference in the world.

I love to be around Christians who are serious about taking God seriously. But I'm retiring from the Christianity that strangles on gnats while the world is choking to death on camels. (Strange analogy from the New Testament—if you don't get it, read Matthew 23:24.)

I hope that kind of Christianity dies, because it doesn't deserve to live if it doesn't take Christ seriously. I'm also ready for its demise because I'm increasingly embarrassed by it all. That's the next reason I'm done with "Christianity."

Reason 4: Christianity Has Become Ridiculous

I mean really. Don't you feel that way most of the time when you watch Christian stuff on television? Is it just me? I'm just so tired of cringing. Now, I say this as one who is on television myself. But if there's any better picture of the strange subculture Christianity has become than Christian television, I don't know what it is. The bizarre hair, the constant appeals for money from people who live in mansions and fly private jets, the glitz and the glamour of those who are supposed to represent the suffering servant who had no place to lay his head, the send-me-your-money-and-you'll-get-rich-and-be-healed scams. When they watch this stuff, the world sees Christianity as some kind of weird sect. And they mock it. If you haven't seen the YouTube video of a certain televangelist supposedly passing gas, watch it. You'll see how ridiculous we look to the world. And you'll laugh too, because it really is funny. Then there are the seemingly constant scandals. As I'm writing this, seven of the most "blessed" television ministries in America are under senate investigation.

It's ridiculous, and yet the money keeps flowing in to these caricatures of faith. Perhaps it's due to a desperate longing among Christians for something real—for the authentic power the Bible talks about. If we don't see it in our normal lives, many will set aside their reason, discernment, and even their money to support the forms of Christianity that claim to provide it—even if it's clearly ridiculous. I just can't be a part of that anymore.

Christianity also seems to have a lock on being the leading organization to oppose almost everything that seems popular and relatively harmless in America.

Teletubbies, look out. We're coming for you. Teenage Mutant Ninja Turtles, take your New Age martial arts back to hell with you. Smurfs—we will crush you! Disney, get that gay mouse away from our children. On and on the silliness goes. I'm ashamed to say that I bought in to a lot of this in my younger years. After all, I wanted to be a member of the club in good standing. Sure am embarrassed about it now, though.

But surely there are some things so dastardly, so hot from the fires of hell, so filled with the essence of evil that Christianity has done the world a huge favor by fighting on God's behalf. One such evil arose from England, and Christians sounded the call to arms.

From the shadows of some dark British castle, or witch's coven, or some such place, came a modern-day Jezebel. Drawing from satanic texts and other such hideous influences, this woman wrote a book. And to seal her fate as the mortal enemy of Christianity and of all things good and pure, she dared to write it for children. She came for our own, to draw them into her web, to seduce them with her demonic ideas. The name of this spawn of Satan?

J. K. Rowling.

And the name of the accursed book?

Harry Potter and the Sorcerer's Stone.

The war has been raging for more than a decade now, and through six sequels. You can still hear the missiles fired from pulpits, at protests, and on many websites. Even the Pope warned about the "subtle seductions" of these evil books. Rowling tells the story of shopping in New York one day with her kids when a man recognized her. This warrior of the faith brought his face close to hers and said, "I'm praying for you," in tones Rowling says "were more appropriate to saying 'Burn in hell,' and I didn't like that 'cause I was with my kids. It was unnerving. If ever I expected to come face to face with an angry Christian fundamentalist, it wasn't in FAO Schwarz."[8]

Doesn't that make you proud to be a Christian?

Well, how has the war against Harry Potter worked out for us?

Rowling has become the second richest woman in entertainment (only Oprah has more money). She's the only person ever to become a billionaire by writing books. The last Harry Potter installment sold 15 million copies worldwide in twenty-four hours, more than *The Da Vinci Code* sold in a year.[9] And the vast majority of the world looked on our brand of Christianity with a mix of mockery and disgust as they made their way to the store for the next book.

But what if the books *are* evil? After all, they must be. Rowling's not one of us, is she? She writes about wizards and spells and stuff like that. Of course, so did Tolkien and Lewis, but that's okay because they were Christians using Christian imagery. They're in our family.

Yet Rowling kept an interesting secret all these years, only to discuss it recently for the first time. It concerns her theme throughout the series.

In the final book, Harry discovers an inscription on his parents' tombstone. Rowling says this inscription "is the theme for the entire series."[10] Here it is: "The last enemy that shall be destroyed is death." In case you don't recognize it, it's 1 Corinthians 15:26 (KJV).

The theme of the entire Harry Potter series is a Bible verse.

It turns out that Rowling says she is a Christian. She had her children christened and attends church regularly. Though she was not raised in a religious family, she became a seeker, attending church alone as a child. She explains, "I was very drawn to faith. . . . I certainly had this need for something that I wasn't getting at home, so I was the one who went out looking for religion."[11]

Great.

Do you get this? While Christianity was waging war on J. K. Rowling, she was seeking Christ the whole time! What if we had befriended her instead of threatening her? What if we had lis-

tened a little before bringing out the big guns? When will we stop
turning our mission field into a battleground? When will we stop
making opponents out of God-seeking friends?

I can already hear the voices of holy soldiers rising in har-
mony: "But she's not a Christian! She's not one of us. She's liberal
in her theology!"

Sure, Rowling probably wouldn't sign the Baptist Faith and
Message doctrinal statement. And she makes it clear that her
purpose is not evangelistic: "I did not set out to convert anyone
to Christianity. I wasn't trying to do what C. S. Lewis did." But
she used the same kind of symbolism that Lewis and Tolkien—
whom we revere—used, and she used it to proclaim a message
that sounds an awful lot like the gospel. "I kept arguing that
'love is the most important force. . . . ' So I wanted to show him
loving. Sometimes it's dramatic: it means you lay down your
life."[12]

Maybe after reading this, you still believe that Harry Potter is
evil.

Fine.

Not my major concern. Maybe you could even convince me
that this kind of thing is evil so that the next time something like
this comes around, I will join your war.

But maybe, in the meantime, we could start doing something
about opposing a few of the devil's other pursuits? Stuff like
genocide, racism, starvation, the mass murder of children before
and after birth, AIDS . . .

Or let's stay really spiritual and concentrate on the Great
Commission for a while.

After we finish healing these gaping wounds the devil is gash-
ing into the hearts of humanity, we might then take a look at the

paper cut of the possible evil of Harry Potter. Or even better, next time we might love someone like J. K. Rowling and trust God to be a big enough boy to defend himself.

Life is too short to invest it in the ridiculous mess we've allowed much of Christianity to become. So I'm looking for something else.

Reason 5: Christianity Has Become a Monument; I'm Looking for a Movement

Two thousand years ago the most profound course change in all of history was the Jesus Movement. I know that we call what happened in the 1960s and '70s the Jesus Movement. I came to Christ because of it. But that was only a small-scale replica of the original. What we know as Christianity began as a spiritual, cultural, transformational movement in which a small group of people who had no means to change anything literally changed the world. They did it by putting aside the many things that could have distracted them—that could have destroyed the movement in its embryonic days—and they just followed Jesus. They did it passionately. They did it sacrificially. They did it missionally. They did it as family.

It wasn't easy, you know. They had far more working against them than we do today, and far less going for them. They had no means of fast communication or rapid transportation. They didn't have the government's favor. They did have an unfortunate burden that Western Christianity doesn't carry these days—they risked being burned alive, sawed in two, crucified, or beheaded. They disagreed amongst themselves, just like we do—sometimes vehemently. But somehow they held it together. Somehow they refused to let it become all about themselves. Somehow they kept it about the commission Jesus had given them.

And the reason they were able to do that?

Because it was *about Jesus.*

These people really believed in God. They really believed he had sent his Son, who had lived for them, died for them, defeated death for them . . . and then sent them out into the world with his message.

They lived like they actually believed in him. Like he was real.

That's what Christianity today is missing. It doesn't resemble a Jesus Movement anymore. Much of it isn't even about Jesus.

Do we need a new Reformation? I've said we do, but that's probably wrong. A reformation implies that there's something at the core that can be reformed, and then all will be well. I'm not sure that the Christianity of today has much more in common with the Jesus Movement than it does with other religions. Would a reformation of Buddhism or Hinduism help us? In fact, I don't believe we need religion at all.

We need Jesus!

So maybe instead of a reformation, we need a reversal. A return to the original Jesus Movement. What would that look like? Well, that's the really cool part of such a Jesus Movement. You don't know for sure. You don't control it. You actually believe in the Holy Spirit, and he leads it. I'm convinced that a lot of what we do has nothing to do with God's Word but much to do with our own traditions and systems. And a move of God's Spirit may very well change all of that. So we would be in for an adventure, a dangerous journey through uncharted waters with many hidden risks.

But how much fun would that be!

To feel the wind of the Spirit in our faces as we run.

To know that we will fail if we keep on doing the same
old stuff.

To know that it must be about Jesus.

To feel the risk and the joy, the significance and the
suffering. The camaraderie of a kingdom movement
that sweeps us along with it.

To catch hold of God like we really believe Matthew
11:12—"The kingdom of heaven has been forcefully
advancing, and forceful men lay hold of it."

To be those men and women who latch onto Christ, even if
it's with our last breath on this earth, and never let go.

To know beyond all doubt that our one shot at life has
been significant.

A Jesus Movement.

Now, a lot of questions remain for me. How exactly do I live
as part of a Jesus movement? I hope the rest of this book will
help me with that even as I write it, and that it will help you a
little too. Whatever else happens, I must leave the broken form
of Christianity to pursue the Jesus Movement. This I know. I'm
looking for others who want to do the same.

The word *Christian* is a good word; a biblical word. It means
"a follower of Christ." I don't reject this word at all. Although,
honestly, I don't use it much anymore because so many people as-
sociate it with the mess we call Christianity. But before we go any
further, I think it would help to clarify our definition of a Christian. What would it look like today to be the kind of Christian
who could join a new Jesus Movement?

I've found a definition I love. It comes from the writings of a great Jesus follower of past days named A. W. Tozer. Here it is: "A Christian is a holy rebel let loose in the world, with access to the throne of God, so that Satan never knows from which direction the danger will come."[13]

I love it. Let's be rebels. We need to be let loose in the world, not defined by what happens within the four walls of our church buildings. We have access to the throne of God. If we believe he is real, let's act like we do. Let's pray like we do. Then we will become dangerous again, coming at the Enemy from every direction—a movement. Not dangerous to children's storybooks and cartoon characters and businesses we don't like. Dangerous to the real author of evil, our real Enemy—who, I believe, is a big fan of "Christianity" but will do all he can to stop a new Jesus Movement.

Here's some good news. The world is ripe for a movement. Postmodernism is beginning to take its toll. A young generation is increasingly nervous about a world with no objective truth, nothing to base their lives on securely. There's a giant void out there waiting to be filled. Don't believe me? Back to Harry Potter then.

I don't care what you think of the books or the author. But no one can deny what has happened. Words on a piece of paper have changed the world. Words written for children. Words bursting with imagination. This is astounding. They're just books. Yet the response to them sounds more like what the church is meant to cause. The books have spawned the Harry Potter Alliance, an online group (www.thehpalliance.org) founded by Andrew Slack, a twenty-eight-year-old from Boston. The group's rallying cry, based on the books, is "The weapon we have is love." When the seventh and final book was released, the Alliance organized rallies from Australia to South America and across the United States to call for action concerning Darfur. *Time* called it a "What Would Harry Do?" campaign. In the days following the rallies, a massive response came from schools signing up to be a part of an antigenocide coalition. Listen to Slack's challenge, which sounds like a passionate gospel sermon: "We can be like Dumbledore's army, who woke the world up to Voldemort's return, and wake our ministries and our world to ending the genocide in Darfur."[14]

If that sounds silly to you, consider the worldwide effect of Harry Potter. The books have been translated into sixty-five languages, "giving people a way to discuss culture and commerce, politics and values," said *Time* magazine writer and editor Nancy Gibbs. Princeton English professor William Gleason likened the impact to that of *Uncle Tom's Cabin,* which "penetrated all levels of society." He believes the Harry Potter books have "spoken profoundly to enough readers that they will be read and reread by children and by adults for a long time."[15]

What an opportunity the church has missed! While we were busy fighting against Harry Potter, we missed a movement that the whole world culture was ready for. Pepperdine University professor of English James Thomas says, "They've made millions of kids smarter, more sensitive, certainly more literate and probably more ethical and aware of hypocrisy and lust for power. They've made children better adults, I think. I don't know of any books that have worked that kind of magic on so many millions of readers in so short a time in the history of publications."[16]

Don't like Harry Potter?

Okay.

What were you doing when this movement began? Why weren't you writing something better? Why are we always opposing and so rarely creating? What Harry Potter has done mirrors what the church is meant to do. And if we don't like it, we have only one place to put the blame.

Christianity.

What has Christianity been up to while the Harry Potter movement spread? I can tell you about some of the meaningful, world-changing debates I've witnessed just in my own denomination since Rowling began writing the series in 1990:

- whether a missionary can have a private prayer language (by the way, if it's private, why is anyone talking about it?);
- whether a missionary had to be baptized not just by immersion but in a Baptist church;
- whether a Catholic could write an article on a Baptist website, even if he was supporting our position;
- whether we should pray with other denominations;
- whether you can be both a Baptist and a Freemason (and whether Freemasons are about to take over the world);
- whether we should clap our hands in church;
- whether black people should be able to join our churches (yes, in this day and age, this is still an issue in many churches, including some I have pastored);
- whether we should lift our hands in worship;
- whether rock music is evil; and of course, the issue we think we can finally solve after centuries of debate,
- whether we have free will or whether God has just

predestined everything so that it all turns out the way
he wants it.

This is a very incomplete list of our many squabbles. When we're
not waging war against Disney and Harry Potter outside the
church, we're busy slashing at each other on the inside. Until we
rebel against this, reject it utterly and start over, all hope is gone.
Because none of this is about Jesus, and he is our only hope.

Movements matter. Institutions are often necessary and are
neither good nor evil in themselves. But institutions do not better
the world. Movements do. And Christianity has become the ultimate institution full of institutions. In *The Shaping of Things to
Come,* Michael Frost and Alan Hirsch discuss the power of cultural movements in the world today, such as Burning Man, the
annual radical self-expression event in the Black Rock Desert of
Nevada. They write, "Unless the church recovers its role as a subversive, missionary movement, no one who has been to Burning
Man will be the least bit interested in it."[17] I agree. A subversive,
rebellious, Spirit-led movement is our only chance.

Surprisingly, I'm hopeful. Let's not forget that our nation was
birthed not long after a spiritual movement. Most scholars agree
that without the First Great Awakening (1730s and 1740s), the
American Colonies would not likely have had the health, moral
fiber, or backbone to stand together against the British. Spiritual
revolution preceded national revolution.

Later, the Second Great Awakening shaped the new country
in positive ways as well. The Prayer Revival of 1857–1858 led to
more than a million conversions and helped sustain both Union
and Confederate armies during the Civil War, and the nation
during Reconstruction. The Welsh Revival of 1904–1905 spread

to the United States and, in fact, nearly worldwide with impact that lasted for decades.

In more recent times, entire nations have been evangelized and massive numbers of people converted in places such as South Korea, which now sends missionaries to America! David Aikman's book *Jesus in Beijing* recounts some of the amazing changes taking place in China because of a Jesus Movement there. And I saw with my own eyes the power of a spiritual movement during my teen years, when the modern Jesus Movement reached all the way from California to the mountains of North Carolina to lead me to Christ.

In 1995 and 1996 I watched a church and a community and more than a hundred college campuses experience a powerful move of God that has come to be called the Brownwood Revival. Seldom does a week go by that I don't hear from some of the thousands affected by that movement who are still making an impact for the kingdom of God all over the world today.

Movements matter.

Can we see a new Jesus Movement in America? Probably not in traditional, institutionalized Christianity as I have described it. It's too absorbed in guarding its turf and protecting its turf lords. Institutions tend to protect themselves at all costs, and I see no sign that the institution of Christianity will move toward Jesus. So I think it has to go in order for revival to come.

But that's not such bad news. Thousands of people are already leaving the institution of Christianity for a better way. Some, like me, have been exiting for a while without really knowing it. But they've left the trappings of Christianity, not Christ or his Church. Indeed, they left to follow Jesus. They want life to count, like it did for those first followers of the Way two thousand years ago. They know that the worst attacks will come from within entrenched Christianity, but they're willing to take the shots. These people will be the start of the rebellion of which I hope to be a part.

So where does this leave me, personally? I'm excited! For now, I have a great, supportive family and a great church that has shown every sign of wanting to be part of a new Jesus Movement. (Hopefully, when they read this book, they still will.)

I also see hope in churches all across America. My comments here are not meant to be a blanket criticism of the church. Thousands of churches are making a difference: loving one another, loving the unlovable, living as though God is real. I am looking toward the future with optimism, hope, and a lot of uncertainty—and, I'll admit, some sadness too. It's hard to leave behind a comfortable past.

But I feel like I've looked behind the curtain and seen the wizard. And the system of Christianity is just not what it's cracked up to be. So I'm taking myself out of the club before my membership can be revoked. That leaves me with just one central driving passion in my life, around which everything else revolves.

Jesus.

I love Jesus. I know I don't love him as I should or even as I want to, but nevertheless, I love him. There are times when his love washes over me, and I feel it as surely as did the centurion who stood beneath the cross, spattered by the Savior's blood, hammer in hand, crying out, "Surely he was the Son of God" (Matthew 27:54).

Recently I attended a revival meeting hosted by the African American churches of our area. Bishop Leo Cyrus spoke about that centurion, and it was nothing short of amazing. He talked about the awesome love of God. And he asked a question I'd never before considered: "Why did God allow Jesus to hang on the cross for so long?" Couldn't he have died for our sins in a few minutes instead of six hours? Is God just into torture, or what? Cyrus wondered aloud if God let his Son suffer so long for the sake of one Roman soldier who was watching. But then the bishop reminded us that the centurion was wrong about one thing. He said that Jesus *was* the Son of God. Cyrus rose up, stood tall, and his voice rang out: "He *is* the Son of God! He *is* the Son of God!"

And he is.

I believe this. I really do. I can do an adequate job of defending my faith. I know the arguments of apologetics. But beyond this, I know God's love, demonstrated through Jesus. I know it. It has covered me, shattered me, broken me, healed me, made me and unmade me, sustained me, and held me.

I believe in Jesus.

I love Jesus.

But I'm done with "Christianity."

Where will all this lead us?

My journey away from Christianity has not led me away from Jesus. In fact, it has led me straight to him. I really believe that if we live as though God is real, Christianity as we know it will die. It's terminally ill, and I can't see a cure.

But Jesus lives. I believe that he will stand on the grave of "Christianity" and beckon us to simply follow him. It is my desire to do so. Many of us are ready to make that pilgrimage together—to follow the real Jesus and to live as though he is real.

I stood at a graveside the other day, as I have hundreds of

times. I had just participated in the funeral of Morris Dupre, a wonderful leader in our church. As the service ended, I hugged his stepdaughter Cindy Cameron, a dear friend of our family. As I did, she pointed down at a tombstone nearby. I was standing next to the grave of her son Jason. Jason had been killed in a terrible accident before I had become pastor of that church.

I stood with my arm around this strong but wounded woman as I read the words of love and truth written on the gravestone. And through eyes glazing with tears, I noticed her husband—Jason's father and my friend, John Cameron—standing directly behind the tombstone. I stepped to him and put my arm around him too. After a moment I said, "We only have a little time here, don't we, John?" He nodded. "It makes me want to really live it. Whatever time he gives us. To make a difference," I said. With steely strength in his eyes and resolve in his voice, John said, "Let's do it. Let's go. Let's go."

And so we went. Out of a cemetery and on into life. A life that matters. A life lived not for a religious institution that's dying but for a God who is living.

A God who is real.

3

If God Were Real . . .
Missionaries Would Lose Their Jobs

Missionless religion that calls itself Christianity is an
affront to God, however it styles itself.
Reggie McNeal, *The Present Future*

THE CHURCH I pastor knows that I pastor as a missionary, so
this is a strange chapter title coming from a guy like me. The
first time I went overseas and saw people begging for a Bible
and leaving their food lines to hear the gospel, I knew God was
calling me. I could not merely pastor a nice church until my
retirement kicked in: I had to be a part of God's mission to the
world. Many of the best moments of my life have been spent
with missionaries:

- sitting beside a missionary in a hut in Southeast Asia
  while people hear the name of Jesus for the first time
  in their lives and watching those same people become
  the first believers in their village.
- working beside missionaries caring for Chernobyl
  children in the former Soviet Union.
- sharing the Lord's Supper with members of an

underground church in Asia and baptizing believers secretly in a hotel bathtub.

- walking through the bazaar in one of the oldest cities on earth beside courageous missionaries in the Middle East.
- eating some of the weirdest stuff you can imagine while sitting beside steel-stomached missionaries who do it all the time.
- celebrating with missionaries over radically changed lives.

Believe me: My problem is not with missionaries. It's with missionless Christianity. It is time for missionaries to lose *their* job because it becomes *our* job. And more than just our job: like for the missionaries who are my heroes, it becomes our *life*.

When a Church Isn't a Church

Author Reggie McNeal states the problem well: "The North American church is suffering from severe mission amnesia. It has forgotten why it exists."[1]

This is a serious matter. In fact, I believe we have to question whether an organization that calls itself a church but shows no evidence of being committed to the mission and commission that Jesus gave to the church is truly a church.

From what we see in the Bible, it does seem possible for a church to be in danger of being rejected as a church by Jesus. In Revelation 2 Jesus warned the church in Ephesus: "I will come to you and remove your lampstand from its place" (v. 5). In chapter 3 things get even worse as he says to the church in Laodi-cea, "I am about to spit you out of my mouth" (v. 16).

If Jesus tells a church what to do and they don't do it, whom to love and they won't love them, why they exist and they don't care, is that group of people really a church? I would argue that many of the churches in America today are fundamentally sick. In my own denomination, a study conducted by LifeWay Christian Resources found that 89 percent of our churches are not healthy. And the clear reason they were unhealthy is that they were reaching few, if any, unchurched people. They had become insular, devoting most of their time and energy to the needs of those already there.

The situation might be at least a little better if we had some atmosphere of emergency in our churches, a desperation to change before it's too late. But as long as our own needs are met, the absence of mission doesn't seem to bother most of our churches.

I often speak at conferences, and I increasingly find myself pleading with churches to change—to see the emergency we're in and act now. Recently, after one such conference, a pastor told me with excitement that his key older leaders had responded pos-itively to my message and were willing to let him make changes to reach younger people and unchurched people. He was shocked because they had shown no interest in this in the past. I agreed to meet with him and help him think through what to do. He de-veloped what seemed to be a wise plan. He would not do any-thing too wild or radical, just start an additional service designed to reach their mission target. He asked the leaders if they would support this, and they said they would. I was excited for him. It's rare to see entrenched church leaders change like this, so I couldn't wait to see the results. They promised their pastor that they would "have his back" if some didn't like the changes.

I should have known better.

Just as I sat down to write this chapter, I received an email from that pastor:

> Just wanted to give you a quick update on how the attempt at change went at [our church]. I carried out all the plans I discussed with you at our meeting. After that meeting, I met with our deacons who were all supportive previously, but I could tell were now more hesitant to proceed. Fears of emotionalism, Pentecostalism, etc. I suggested a Destiny prayer service [that's our Wednesday night service, where we actually pray like God is real] before our revival services, and that was just too weird for them. We had a guy from your church come and lead in worship that week of revival, and he did a great job of blending the two styles. Yet, in the end, it was too contemporary for the older crowd and too traditional for the youth. . . . God began directing my heart and passions about a year ago to do things that I now see are not compatible with [this church]. The revival and worship attempt only confirmed what my wife and I had been sensing—the end of our ministry here.

I feel sick . . . again. I've felt sick like this so many times in recent years that the illness has become chronic. Think about what happened in this "church." First, they misled their pastor, saying they were willing to support change . . . until it was actually time to make the changes. Second, they were concerned about "emotionalism and Pentecostalism" but seemingly unconcerned about the soon-coming death of their church. Third, any service that involved actually praying for people other than themselves was apparently so foreign to them that it struck them as "weird." Fourth, even though the music was not contemporary enough to appeal to a younger crowd, they still rejected it as too different from what they liked. Finally, they are willing to lose a wonderful young pastor to maintain their status quo. It's all about them. They have, in essence, told the whole mission field in which they live to go to hell. Does this "church" really qualify any longer as a church?

McNeal describes perfectly the state most of our churches are in: "A lot of religious clubs (currently called churches) will continue to operate just fine—for a while, maybe a long while, depending on how well they build and manage their endowment. It is quite possible that we will have a number of churches being financed by dead people. As long as missionless churches maintain financial support, they can remain in their denial and self-delusion that they are the Christian movement in North America."[2]

This is the ultimate example of living as though God were not real! If we believe what Jesus said when he gave the Great Commission, how can anyone claim to be his follower and yet be willing to stand before him one day having opposed his mission?

The really amazing thing is that if you asked people in many of these churches about missions, they would claim that their church was "very missions-minded." That usually means that they give some money to missions. They might even send some people on short-term mission trips or support a missionary from their church. But one glaring element is missing in the mission of these churches: they almost completely ignore the mission field where they live.

I illustrated this in a message I preached at a conference recently. I gave the people a simple way to judge whether their church was really committed to missions. I said, "If you have a missionary come and tell you a story of reaching hundreds of children with AIDS in Africa, you'll cry and applaud. But what will happen in your church, right where you live, if your pastor brings in hundreds of African Americans? Or hundreds of people with AIDS?" Awkward silence filled the room.

The whole world has changed around us. Every church sits in the middle of a mission field. The diversity of races, cultures, religions, philosophies, and worldviews has grown so rapidly that it's shocking.

You live on the mission field!

But the truth is that most of Christianity is not terribly interested in Jesus' mission. Fulfilling that mission would require so much change from the current club regulations that one thing becomes clear to the doorkeepers: if they let this change in, the club will never be the same. It will not even resemble what it has been. And that's just too much to bear.

So we appoint a professional class of missionaries to do the dirty work for us—and we make sure that the dirty work they do stays far enough from the front doors of our church buildings to avoid the nasty reminder that we ourselves are supposed to be doing something on this mission. We either celebrate the missionaries as distant heroes or, just as often, forget that they're even out there at all. Either way, we're free of the burden.

From Missions as Job to Missional DNA

We distance ourselves even further from the mission of Jesus by forming "mission agencies." That way a group of "experts" in a building somewhere can handle all the missionary stuff so our churches can carry on, undistracted, with a host of internal programs and projects. But in its essence, isn't a church supposed to be a mission agency?

I'm not arguing that we should abandon mission agencies. There's strength in a cooperative approach that allows churches to link their efforts and their resources to accomplish more than they could separately. But having served in one of my denomination's mission agencies, I have to question whether that's actually happening. I worked with some of the best people in the world at the North American Mission Board. But the truth is, we knew that much of what we were doing was ineffective. Some good things were happening, but even with all the resources of the largest denomination in evangelicalism behind us, we weren't making the slightest dent in the unchurched population of North America. We were so removed from the average church that most of them never knew or really cared what we were doing. We worked with other good ministries, such as state conventions and local associations, but rarely was there even an effort at real synergy or communication. Even our missionaries felt disconnected from us.

I'll never forget speaking at a missions conference in Alabama. Organizers had brought in missionaries from around the world. I was talking to one of our missionaries who served in North America and asked if she felt supported by our agency. She smiled sadly and said, "I don't know if anyone at the agency really knows we are there." She told me a story of tremendous struggles she and her husband had faced in the previous two years of their work. She said that every month she submitted a report about what they were doing. Because she never got any response, she began to doubt that anyone was even reading them. So, on a day when they were feeling particularly disconnected, she put that to the test. She wrote on their form, "We are in deep despair and intend to blow our brains out!"

They're still waiting for a response.

Looking back on my time on the mission board, I'm not sure how much mission work I actually did. Most of our time seemed to be spent debating how many fine points of the Bible had to be adhered to by people before they could become missionaries, and were the current missionaries actually keeping the rules, and did we have any Catholics writing anything on our website, and was there anyone out there getting any money from us who was drinking wine with his dinner, and were we associating with the "emerging church," and who was allowed to speak to the press, and was our latest restructuring effective?

I wish I could say that I'm exaggerating, but that's pretty much the way it is. Many of us have suggested, even pleaded, for years for a complete overhaul of the way we do missions, the way we spend money, and the way our agencies function. But that has largely fallen on deaf ears. Our efforts at change and restructuring have done little but rearrange the deck chairs on the *Titanic*. It's just so hard for institutional Christianity to do anything but protect itself, defend the system, and guard the positions of the power brokers.

Honestly, I hate to write these things. I still pastor a church affiliated with the Southern Baptist Convention. Our church is one of the largest missions-giving churches in our Convention. I haven't given up hope for renewal within this denomination. But I'm not holding my breath either. And I'm learning a new freedom that comes from sharing life with the broader kingdom of God. A lot can be learned from other Christ followers who are not from my own tradition. It's nice to be free to learn from them without the constant suspicion of heresy hanging over my head.

I love Southern Baptists. I owe many good things in my life to these wonderful people. But I admit to a deep disappointment with what I've seen take place in my tenure in the largest sect of evangelical Christianity—and a real fear for the future if something doesn't change radically . . . and fast.

So I'm moving on from the failed-mission mess we've called Christianity.

And the really sad thing is that many missionaries are moving on too, or trying to figure out how. They desperately want to be missionaries, but they didn't sign on for the bureaucratic, cumbersome hindrances we keep putting in their way. They're willing to give their lives for Jesus but not for a trustee board. So as I talk to missionaries these days, it's rare that I find any who are not rolling their eyes at the mess we've made. And many are actively seeking a way out—ironically, so they can actually be involved in missions again.

Some of our best friends are leaving their positions after fifteen years of faithful service. Their reason?

"We just can't do this with integrity anymore. So much money is spent for agency people to fly in and tell us what rules we have to keep that we don't have money to actually do the work. If people knew what we knew, they wouldn't give any money at all. We have to get out of this for the sake of our faith."

Simultaneously, many missionaries are staying, and many more are going. I'm not criticizing these missionaries in the least, but I am questioning the system we've created. If we really believed in God and all he has told us, our current view of the "missionary" would make no sense.

If we really believed God, everyone would be in on the mission!

In fact, I believe that the mission would be the very core of the church's DNA. No follower of Christ would be able to make any sense out of a life lived apart from the mission of loving, serving, and sharing the good news with those who are not yet followers of Christ. Many would still move to other countries as "missionaries." But those who stayed here would never see themselves as any less called to the mission. And every church would see its role as a mission agency.

Our present concept of missionaries—a special few whose professional job is to take the gospel to other cultures in faraway places—would make no sense. Not if we truly believe God is real.

So what are we to do? Unless we have some plan, some path forward, then all I'm doing is whining.

And I hate whiners.

So let me offer my thoughts—what I'm sure will be a woefully incomplete and flawed strategy, but at least, I hope, a faint trail through the wilderness ahead that I intend to travel until someone shows me a better route.

Leaving Christianity for the Mission Field

My friend Ed Stetzer, coauthor of wonderful books such as *Breaking the Missional Code* and *Comeback Churches,* calls believers to live missional lives. That's *mission* as an adjective: letting your life be defined, described, directed, and encircled by the mission. When I first heard Ed use that phrase, I felt that I could see through the thick undergrowth of the forest of Christianity for the first time in a long time. This was what I was after. Many others are writing about missional thinking and living these days too, and that gives me great hope. Of course, like anything that threatens the norms of the Christianity club, all kinds of controversy surround the term *missional.* That in itself should tell us a lot about Christianity's sickness. How in the world can we make living a life defined by mission controversial?

But enough of that discussion. How do we do it? Not just me or you: how do we see a missional movement in the church? How do we see something in our time that actually resembles a Jesus Movement? I'm not trying to present a comprehensive plan for fulfilling the Great Commission. If I were doing that, I wouldn't even start with the American church. Given the explosive growth of the church in the Third World, it seems that's the most promising arena for that kind of plan. If we want the kind of movement I've talked about in this book, is there anything we can do about it? I think so. Here are three steps toward starting a Jesus Movement that will help us fulfill the Great Commission:

1. Face the Awful and Exciting Truth

The awful truth is that the vast majority of the churches of Christianity are not going to survive. As I've already mentioned, many appear not to be churches anymore anyway. Many more are only one more split or a few more funerals away from their demise. I no longer believe that we should waste time trying to save these churches. I've stopped urging young pastors to "stay for the long haul" as many encourage them to do. I suggest that, if their church is insular and abstaining from the actual mission of Jesus, they take a short time to find out if the people are willing to change. If not, these ministers should move on to a "real" church or be a part of starting one. I see no reason gifted leaders called by God should waste their lives on "the long haul" if what that means is hauling a rotting corpse around like a ball and chain. Life is too short for that. I believe this to be the truth.

But that truth is not all awful. It also means that God is entrusting the advance of his kingdom to a relative few. Those who are willing to actually follow him have the potential to make a big impact.

If you are a follower of Christ, determined to live as though God is real, you have the opportunity to experience much of what it must have felt like to be a first-century believer. You are a pioneer, an intrepid adventurer launching into the unknown with a message of hope for a world that, like two thousand years ago, is largely ignorant of that message.

And if you're a leader—a pastor or other minister, a church planter, a missionary, or any other leader on this journey—God has placed the future of the church in your hands.

I know that the church is ultimately in God's hands. But throughout Scripture (and history), we see that God uses leaders: human leaders. He entrusts frail, fallen, but full-of-wild-faith people to lead his eternally significant movements.

Now that's cool. And that's where we are.

This time should be as exciting for us as it was for one group of soldiers a long time ago. Imagine that you're minding your own business, just getting a drink of water from the river along with 9,999 other soldiers, and you happen to lap the water up with your hands instead of kneeling down to drink straight from the river. And on that basis you're chosen as one of only three hundred who are allowed to embark on a mission to fight the enemy.

And you kicked their butts!

Sure, it would be great to be part of an army of ten thousand that won that battle. But three hundred? That's something to remember for the rest of your life.

You may feel as randomly selected as the soldiers Gideon chose in Judges 7. But here you are. You are chosen. Once you've faced this lonely but energizing truth, you're ready to move. But move where?

2. Move into Humility

If we're looking for a starting point for getting in on a new movement of God, and we actually believe he is real, I assume we would want to do what he says—especially when he says it over and over.

"This is the one I esteem: he who is humble and contrite in spirit" (Isaiah 66:2).

"'God opposes the proud but gives grace to the humble.' Humble yourselves, therefore, under God's mighty hand, that he may lift you up in due time" (1 Peter 5:5–6).

If I want to be esteemed by God, if I want the grace of God to be active around me, if I want to see God's mighty hand at work, and if I don't want to end up being opposed by God, I must humble myself.

I don't particularly like that as a starting point. I'd rather develop a strategic plan, preach to a big stadium of leaders, move into a new paradigm, and every other thing we've been trying for a long time that lets me be up front.

But Jesus keeps getting in the way.

"Jesus called them together and said, 'You know that the rulers of the Gentiles lord it over them, and their high officials exercise authority over them. Not so with you. Instead, whoever wants to become great among you must be your servant, and whoever wants to be first must be your slave'" (Matthew 20:25–27).

Not so with you.

But it *is* so with me.

And that scares me. Because if I understand correctly what God is saying, I can lead a great church, speak to great conferences, hold key positions, even write a book that lots of people read—and never even enter the arena of the movement of God.

Unless I want to be humble.

It seems to me that no one naturally wants to be humble. It flies in the face of all of our personal desires and even a lot of what we've been taught in Christianity. And maybe that's why we see so little of the power of the Spirit in this country. Maybe in other places, believers are first and foremost hungry for God. But most of the time, it seems I'm just hungry for God to do for me what I want. And that's a big difference.

Every time God moves in a powerful, visible, and transformational way, he starts with a humble man or woman who listens to him and talks to him.

He started with Moses, who would have made a lousy megachurch pastor because he had no confidence at all to stand before people and talk. But the Bible calls him "more humble than anyone else on the face of the earth" (Numbers 12:3).

He started with Joshua, who easily could have revolted against Moses. Joshua was a powerful warrior, and the people might have followed him. But he was content to be Moses' aide until "the LORD exalted Joshua in the sight of all Israel" (Joshua 4:14).

He started with Mary, a frightened young teenager, to launch the movement to save mankind. And she sang to him, "He has been mindful of the humble state of his servant" (Luke 1:48).

He started with John the Baptist, the man everyone wanted to hear preach but who directed their attention away from himself and said of Jesus, "He must become greater; I must become less" (John 3:30).

He started with Peter, who, when he preached at Pentecost, saw thousands of souls flock to the kingdom of God, launching the Jesus Movement that changed history. Remarkable, since only weeks before, Peter could be found weeping and running, completely humbled by his own failure and denial of Christ.

The list goes on and on. God chooses the humble to do his great works. And rather than immediate success and accolades, the reward for the kind of humility God uses seems to be adversity.

Maybe the key to being a part of a movement of God is deciding that I really want to be part of it!

Am I willing to endure hatred and rebellion like Moses? Am I willing to wander in the desert for all those years like Joshua? Am I willing to be publicly humiliated like Mary? Am I willing to be utterly broken like Peter? And am I willing even to get my head chopped off like John the Baptist?

Maybe there just isn't a long line of people in this country who really want a movement of God. But such people are out there in the world. I've been with them; seen their sacrifice, their courage, and their humble joy through it all. And when I come home, it makes me more aware of why we aren't seeing God move here. We really don't want what has to happen in us to get us ready for him to move.

These humble people in the Bible seem to be the ones who really listen to God. They may be thickheaded like Peter at first, but they finally learn to hear God—and to talk with him.

And that leads me to a conclusion that seems so obvious that it shouldn't need to be mentioned. But in light of the state of the church in North America, nothing else matters compared to this:

3. The Church Must Learn to Pray Again

I mean, really, could anything be more clear? If we really believe in God, maybe we should consider listening to him and talking to him. Doesn't it seem to you that we would need a waiting list to get into our prayer meetings if we actually believed that the creator of the universe would meet us there and communicate with us? But I've only been in a handful of churches in my entire life where I felt that the people actually believed in God this way. I pastor a church that seems to be headed in that direction. But the one church that stands out to me where people pray like they believe in God is the Brooklyn Tabernacle in New York.

The pastor, Jim Cymbala, is my good friend. He's a humble man who listens and talks to God and teaches others to do the same. I've been to his church many times, but I've never been there on a Sunday. Yet I've seen all I need to know about this church to say it's the closest thing I have seen to what happened in the book of Acts. To reach that conclusion, all I needed to see was their Tuesday-night prayer meeting. What happens there is not hype or mere emotion. It's hunger. Desperate hunger. Here's how Jim describes it:

> During countless Tuesday night prayer meetings I find myself encircled by the sacred sounds of prayer and intercession filling the church, spilling into the vestibule, and overflowing from every heart present. As the meeting edges to a close, I overhear mothers petitioning for wayward children . . . men asking God to please help them find employment . . . others giving thanks for recent answers to prayer . . . tearful voices here and there. I can't help but think, *This is as close to heaven as I will ever get in this life. I don't want to leave here. If I were invited to the White House to meet some dignitary, it would never bring the kind of peace and deep joy I sense here in the presence of people calling on the Lord.*[3]

Sounds like a church that actually believes in God. When I've been with these wonderful people, I sense all that Jim describes and more. It's clear that people come with a sense of excitement that they can meet with God, an expectation of what he will do.

And he's doing a lot. Brooklyn Tabernacle is making a transformational difference in that part of the New York City area. Lives are being changed in every imaginable way. People are set free from drug abuse. People who come from every kind of perversion and a multitude of disastrous choices are loved unconditionally. Hundreds graduate each year from their Downtown Learning Center, having been changed in every way: their economic condition is changed; their marriages and parenting are changed; they are spiritually transformed. And believers come from churches all over the world to see what's happening. It's a movement of God.

And I believe that a transformational movement of those who really believe in God is our only hope.

The church I now pastor, First Baptist Church of West Monroe, Louisiana, is starting to believe that too. We're just getting started, but it's becoming clear to us where the power for what's happening here comes from. We meet every Wednesday night for a time together that we call Destiny. We seek to praise and worship Jesus as though we believe he's actually with us. We cry out to him for the overwhelming needs in our community. Hundreds of people come to Christ and are baptized every year in our church, but our people have begun to grasp the possibility of something even bigger—the chance to see transformational change in the community around us, the advance of the kingdom of heaven Jesus talked so much about. So we pray—really pray— for needs we don't know how to meet. We openly pray over people in every kind of disastrous situation. We gather around them, love them, and let them know that they have a family. We ask our heavenly Father to intervene in their lives.

And we're seeing people set free from anorexia, drug and alcohol abuse, family abuse, the chains of horrible experiences in their pasts, and so much more. Almost every week we hear of some financial need that we have no idea how to meet. Invariably, the need somehow gets met. Then we share these things with our people the next week, and their faith grows. We pray for

God to draw to himself people who don't yet know him. One man we prayed for, who is prominent in the community, called me the following day, and before the week was out, I was privileged to lead both him and his wife to Christ.

When I first came to our church and talked about how we as a fellowship would begin to pray, I said something that shocked them. I told them, "We're going to come together and ask God to do miraculous things. And if he doesn't, we're going to become atheists and quit wasting our time here and go play a lot more golf."

Does that shock you the way it shocked some of them? Now, we never demand that God do anything our way. He is God. But he has made many incredible promises, and his Word tells us that he "is able to do immeasurably more than all we ask or imagine" (Ephesians 3:20). I didn't say it. God's Word says it. So we have decided to take God at his word. If he says he will do something, we have decided to trust him. We are learning to come to church expecting God to work. We need a movement of God more than the air we breathe. So we are asking in faith and daily watching for his answers.

Jim Cymbala writes about how movements of God begin:

If our churches don't pray, and if people don't have an appetite for God, what does it matter how many are attending the services? How would that impress God? Can you imagine the angels saying, "Oh, your pews! We can't believe how beautiful they are! Up here in heaven, we've been talking about them for years. Your sanctuary lighting—it's so clever. The way you have steps coming up to the pulpit—it's wonderful. . . ."

I don't think so.

. . . When I stand at the Judgment Seat of Christ, he is not going to ask me if I was a clever orator. He is not going to ask me how many books I wrote. He is only going to ask whether I continued in the line of men and women, starting way back in the time of Adam's grandchildren, who led others to call upon God.[4]

I think Jim is right. I think that's really just about all that matters. In fact, I intended to write a lot more in this chapter. I have an outline in front of me filled with points of strategic planning and missiology. It seems to me to be a pretty good mission plan. But I'm not going to write any of it down. Because if I do, I may be guilty of joining the crowded jumble of "plans" to turn around the mess we're in. Maybe my plan is better than other plans out there. In fact, maybe my plan is the best plan you would have ever heard. Probably not, but it doesn't matter, because you're not going to hear any of it from me. The truth is that it seems, based on accounts in the Bible, that our plans aren't supposed to work. Moses' plan didn't work. He needed God's plan. Peter's plan didn't work. He needed God's plan. Mary had no plan. She needed God's plan. And John the Baptist? Maybe Jesus called him great because all he seemed to want was God's plan! So he rambled around the desert eating bugs and generally acting like a guy we would put on Prozac, and yet he fulfilled prophecy, prepared the way for Jesus, and played his part in the redemptive plan for mankind.

God's plan. It's the only one we need.

And I just can't find any other way for us to get in on the right plan—God's plan—than to humble ourselves, give up our own plans, and then pray—really pray—and ask God to show us his.

Just last night I spoke at a conference where black and white followers of Christ were meeting together. We had a great time. God met us there. We left feeling a renewed passion to follow God. A key leader in our community was present. He came to me afterward, in tears, and said, "Do you know how hard it is to realize that you have been doing the wrong thing all your life?" Now, I don't know what exactly he needed to change; but I know that his humility and brokenness is exactly what we all need. I saw his pain, the realization of wasted time, but I also saw in him the possibility of something wonderful that he did not see at the moment. And I told him what I saw. That perhaps now he was in exactly the right place, the place of brokenness and humility to see God's plan enacted in his life as never before.

If this all sounds a little too theoretical to you, not enough practical steps to take, I understand. But again, I urge you to watch God at work in the history he has given us in his Word. He doesn't seem too interested in making sense to us. He wants to know if we believe him enough to follow him—and to expect that what he has done before, he can and will do again.

How does the mission get accomplished? It's not complex. Consider this:

What if every city had a Brooklyn Tabernacle? Just one. If every other church in every city decided to continue with their religious club activities, but just one chose to really believe God, to really follow him in humility, and to really listen to him and talk to him until he moved in power, the mission of Jesus would be accomplished. Our cities would be changed. The Great Commission would be fulfilled.

How can I say this with such certainty? Because we are followers of Christ, and it's our story! It already happened—long ago in Antioch, Philippi, Ephesus, Rome, and Thessalonica. Because one church changed those cities and so many more, eventually the gospel came to your city, to your life. To you. This is what it was like:

> We know, brothers loved by God, that he has chosen you, because our gospel came to you not simply with words, but also with power, with the Holy Spirit and with deep conviction. You know how we lived among you for your sake. You became imitators of us and of the Lord; in spite of severe suffering, you welcomed the message with the joy given by the Holy Spirit. And so you became a model to all the believers in Macedonia and Achaia. The Lord's message rang out from you not only in Macedonia and Achaia—your faith in God has become known everywhere. . . . You turned to God from idols to serve the living and true God, and to wait for his Son from heaven, whom he raised from the dead—Jesus, who rescues us from the coming wrath. (1 Thessalonians 1:4–10)

So go and be a part of that one church in your city. If there are more than one, even better! If there's not even one, help start one. And believe God again.

Reggie McNeal thinks the church in America has forgotten why it exists. He's right. And it's time to remember. He also said: "Jesus has promised that hell will not be able to stand against it [the church]. I just wish hell were the problem."[5]

He's right again.

We are the problem.

God is the answer.

Simple as that. As long as we keep sending missionaries far away to do our work and thinking we have obeyed God, we'll keep being the problem. But maybe, just maybe, we'll open our eyes, take a hard look at where we really are, and realize that it just doesn't make sense. Not if God is real. If he is, and if you intend to follow him . . .

Welcome to the mission field.

4

If God Were Real . . .
Our Family Life Would Shock the World

If your father and mother, your sister and brother, if the
very cat and dog in the house, are not happier for your
being Christian, it is a question whether you really are.
Hudson Taylor

THE FAMILY LIVES of Christians have indeed sometimes shocked
the world, but usually for all the wrong reasons. Shouldn't the
world be shocked if we claim that the creator of the universe lives
in us and yet that seems to make little difference in our homes?

We've all heard the statistics that indicate that divorce rates
are no different among Christians than among those who don't
believe. But things are even worse than that. The truly Christian
family has become such an anomaly in contemporary culture that
many unchurched people view that model as an unrealistic uto-
pian ideal from years gone by that doesn't exist at all anymore—if
it ever did.

Our family embarked on a cruise a few years ago for our vacation. When we were standing in line to get on the ship, we noticed something that seemed pretty unusual. In line in front of us
was a family that appeared to be Amish. I had visited Amish

country before and appreciated the beautiful simplicity, so I'm not bashing the Amish. They just looked . . . well, out of place. The mom, dad, and kids boarding the cruise ship were dressed as though they were about to go bring in the harvest. Through the week we saw them many times, even spoke to them once. Really nice people. But the sight of them sitting around the pool dressed like that is still a little hard to reconcile—or get out of my mind.

During the cruise, one day we were looking for a picture that the ship's photographers had taken of our family—you have to look through everyone's pictures to find yours—and there was the Amish family's picture. It looked as though time travelers had landed on the ship.

Now, I don't know what the rules are concerning the Amish and cruise ships. I don't know if it's completely normal for them to take cruises or if these were rebellious Amish. But it struck me that for most of the Western world, the experience of seeing a committed Christian family is about as foreign as our seeing the Amish on that ship. I don't think that fact has really dawned on most of us—that much of the influence of the Christian home has disappeared from the scene or is so hidden from the sight of the rest of the world that it makes little difference.

I experienced the reality of this a few years ago when my daughter Christi was acting in a show that ran all summer in an outdoor amphitheater. All of the cast lived in the same apartment complex and got to know one another well. The rest of our family went to visit for a week and rented a condo. One day we invited the cast over for a meal and a swim. We had a great time meeting all these talented young actors, but we could tell that they were a little taken aback by our family. After they left, Christi told us that several of them had asked questions that went something like this:

"Was that real? I mean, the whole Mom and Dad around the dinner table thing? Did you really grow up that way?"

Many of them had no experience of anything like that, either in their own upbringing or in witnessing that of their friends. The guys were particularly curious about what it was like to grow up with a father in the house who actually stayed—and where the rest of the family was glad that he did. David Kinnaman says in his book, *unChristian,* "When Christians talk about a heavenly Father who loves us and provides for us, it is a foreign concept to many."[1]

Our failure to provide a visible picture of families who actually follow Jesus has created a vacuum that pop culture has filled with parody. Since most people never see a Christian family in action, they're largely blank slates on which pop culture is only too eager to draw an unflattering caricature. Take for instance that stellar example of Christian values, the Simpsons.

The Simpsons claim to be a Christian family. They attend church. They occasionally talk about God. They pray. But they're clueless. Consider these quotes from our "typical" Christian family:

Lisa Simpson: "I don't know who or what God is exactly, all I know is He's a force more powerful than Mom and Dad put together, and you owe Him big."[2] So the cartoon Christian family that the world has come to see as reality has no coherent idea who God is and really doesn't even try to impart his values to their children.

Bart Simpson: "So we get bored someplace else every Sunday. Does this really change our day to day lives?"[3] That one isn't even funny; just a pretty accurate picture of the family experience in typical Christianity.

This last one is funny, though. Homer Simpson: "Oh, Lord, be honest! Are we the most pathetic family in the universe or what!"[4]

Funny. And scary. Maybe the caricature is not too far from reality. Compared with what we could be, what we are meant to be, what we should be if God is real, maybe we *are* the most pathetic family in the universe.

Maybe we who are called the church are a pathetic family of pathetic families. But the story of the gospel is the story of change: dramatic, impossible, transformational change. I guess the real question is whether we want to be changed.

Recently I was with Donna for my Friday night rite of radical manhood—I was taking her to the latest torture—er, romantic comedy that she was excited about seeing. About a minute into these movies, I can usually tell you how it's going to end. (Guys, I've tried sharing that knowledge with Donna, and let me offer you this advice: it's not a good plan for your date night.) I also can tell early into most of our date movies that I won't see any car chases; no one is going to get shot; nor will any of the other stuff happen that I think makes a movie worth watching. So I was surprised that this one we were watching was actually pretty good. It's called *Enchanted*. Although I could predict how it would end almost from the beginning, at least the way it got there was creative.

The main character, Giselle, is a beautiful young princess in a fairy-tale world, waiting for her prince to come and marry her. But suddenly she is ejected from the fairy tale by her evil mother-in-law-to-be witch and lands in modern-day, real-life Manhattan. There she meets Robert, a divorce lawyer, who is pretty freaked out when birds, cockroaches, rats, and other assorted animals follow her around—and she seems to need to sing a lot. Of course, you can figure out that they eventually fall in love and live happily ever after.

But the really mind-blowing part of the movie, for me, was when Robert tries to explain divorce to Giselle. He helps her to see that in real life, people fall out of love and leave each other. She can't comprehend this. She's shocked. She is grieved. I was stunned to see Hollywood portray the attitude that Christ followers should have toward the disintegration of the family. We should be crushed by the state of the Christian family today. We are concerned, and rightfully so, about issues such as homosexual marriage and abortion. Yet we in the church seem to display much less grief and concern about our own marriages coming apart and the abortion of our families. In the family, God has given an awesome gift to us: the chance to love and be loved, to share life together, to be loaned life in the form of children to shape for significance in this world. He has given us a chance to be a picture of the church—the bond between Christ and his bride. The fact that we can accept the current state of things without even much of a fight—is there any clearer evidence that we live as though God is not real?

I believe that all of this can change. If I believe in God at all, I have to believe that. Again, the real question is, do we want it to change? And if so, what do we do?

Reignite a Vision of What Family Can Be

Ever been to a family reunion? We all know what that's like, don't we? If you looked up *family reunion* in the dictionary, you might expect to find a definition something like "mind-numbing boredom." Standing around with weird Uncle Fred . . . listening to annoying Aunt Bertha gossip . . . watching Grandpa Methuselah drool and snore . . . We can all relate to that, right?

I can't.

I believe in my family as the legacy bearers of biblical passion. Our family is sure not perfect, and we have our quirks like everybody else; but I never think of our family as boring. I believe in God. I believe his Word. So why would I ever think of family life as boring? Have you read the Bible? It's hard to find a boring family story in there. We see plenty of mess-ups and challenges, but not much boredom.

- An old man like Abraham embarks on long journeys of faith with his whole clan.
- A young man like Joseph moves from disaster to disaster to wild success and family renewal.
- Noah's family saves the world!
- Joseph and Mary's family nurtures the Savior of our souls.

We live as though we think these stories are fairy tales. If they are real, then they should be our model, our motivation, and our inheritance.

Family reunions should be fun! They should be like war councils, victory celebrations, treasure hunts, and travelogues. Anything but the boring stereotype.

Donna and I decided even before we were married that we were going to pursue that spiritually adventuring kind of family. We've often failed, but it hasn't been for lack of trying—or for lack of believing that this is what family is meant to be. We've committed together to take this faith journey as a family and to constantly keep the true nature of our mission before our children.

On the inside of a ring Donna gave me for our twenty-fifth wedding anniversary is the engraving "John 15:5." That verse says, "I am the vine; you are the branches. If a man remains in me and I in him, he will bear much fruit; apart from me you can do nothing."

We are in hard pursuit of a family life that is grafted to the life and mission of Jesus. When we live there, it's awesome. When we step away on our own, it's awful. But we believe in God together, and we long to live that way as a family. I'll let Christi give you a glimpse of what that was like:

Growing Up with the Real God
CHRISTI AVANT WATSON

An unknown genius has said, "Families are like fudge, mostly sweet with some nuts." My family is more like peanut brittle; if you take away the nuttiness, we're just a sticky, brittle mess. When I asked seventeen-year-old Trey, the youngest of our family, his thoughts on growing up in the Avant household, he remarked, "Well it has been interesting—kind of loony, but incredible at the same time. Now that I am getting older, I am realizing that our family isn't normal. In some ways I've felt sheltered, but then again, I went to Africa when I was eleven. It's like we have the perfect imperfect family."

Trey could not have said it any better. Both Amy and I, the eldest of the three siblings, walked through that same door of awakening when it became clear that our family was, to say the least, atypical. In 1 Peter 2:11 and in other places in Scripture, followers of Christ are referred to as "aliens and strangers" in the world. If a family has decided to collectively embrace the path of Jesus Christ, they *should* appear a bit odd when compared to those who do not follow Christ. However, as my siblings and I matured, we realized that while our list of don'ts was pretty standard for a typical Christian family, the Avant family list of dos made us weird even compared with other Christian families. Apparently, our parents worshiped and introduced us to a very different God than the two-dimensional, black-and-white, religious god so many families around us seemed to take out for show on Sunday but then brush aside for the rest of the week—families who laid claim to the same faith we did!

When each of us Avant kids turned eleven, we were sent to an underprivileged foreign country for a week or two. Trey, as he said, went to Africa and used simple "magic" tricks to prove to hundreds of villagers that their witch doctor had been deceiving them at the price of their health—and sometimes their lives. Amy went to Belarus and, later, to the Middle East, where she cared for Bedouin women and their children. Not long after freedom of religion had been restored, I went to the former Soviet Union and had to be literally hoisted out of a mob in the market when people, ravenous for God's Word, bum-rushed our group for free Bibles. Most parents threaten to send their kids to Third World countries if they don't behave; mine actually did this as a reward!

Every morning, before school, the family met around the kitchen table for breakfast, and my dad would read reports about individuals giving their lives to serve starving children in Haiti or businesspeople in Hong Kong, and we would pray as if we expected God to listen. As a teenager, rising thirty minutes earlier than necessary for this ritual seemed an atrocity, but now I miss those droopy-eyed times tremendously. I recognize that these "abnormalities" were the building blocks of a family that strives for something infinitely greater than just identifying with a religious system. Most friends I know whose parents raised them "religiously" have stepped away from their religion completely, and I don't blame them. The religion of Christianity isn't helpful when it comes to the quintessential questions about life and the universe that my generation is adamantly asking. The God I grew up with is an active answer to those questions, and yet he's the ultimate mystery. The God I grew up with is Truth, but he's not afraid of doubt. The God I grew up with is supernatural and yet as real as my fingers clacking away on the computer keyboard.

Don't get the wrong idea. As Trey pointed out, our family is not perfect. Yet in their imperfection, my parents taught me raw passion, gritty tenacity, irrepressible romance, unconditional love, and most importantly, the value of letting God be perfect so that I don't have to waste precious seconds of life straining to reach a branch infinitely higher than my arms are long—so that in my personal flaws, I can embrace a world that craves a flawless God.

That has been the journey of our family, and as far as I can see from everything that God says, we're not supposed to be unusual. This can be and should be your family's journey too.

Make the Vision Your Reality

I'd love to give you three easy steps to making your family the sort of family that will cause the world to stand up and take notice that God is real. But we all know that nothing of such great value will be easy. The three steps that follow aren't exercises that will perfect your family through practice, like stomach crunches or aerobic exercise. Instead, these steps require a fundamental change of your perspective and your heart. As Romans 12:2 urges Christ followers: "Do not conform any longer to the pattern of this world, but be transformed by the renewing of your mind." Renewing your mind—and your family—in these three ways will transform your family life . . . which will, in turn, transform the world.

1. Make Your Marriage Missional

If every Christ follower is supposed to be about the mission of Jesus, why would we think that he would join two of us together and not intend to multiply the missional impact? We've completely bought in to the Hollywood, culturally defined view of love and marriage. We get married because we feel so good about this person we met. We just know that we couldn't be happy without him or her. We've found the one to fulfill all our dreams. We'll spend our lives gazing into each other's eyes and find total fulfillment in just being together.

Sounds like another of Donna's movies.

Now, an element of that is true: marriage can often be filled with romance and tenderness, passion and joy. But that's not its purpose! If it is, we're in big trouble. No marriage stays that way all the time. Every marriage—including mine—has moments when we wake up, look at that person in the bed beside us, and think . . . *ew.* When we expect the Hollywood ideal of perpetual romance, we set ourselves up for perpetual disappointment—and for divorce. If we believe love is a feeling, when that feeling is gone, we will be too. That's the reason our divorce rates are no different from the world's—because we think the same way the world thinks about marriage.

Marriage is fundamentally about commitment, not feeling. It's the model Jesus chose to illustrate his relationship with us, the Church, the bride of Christ. The greatest love ever demonstrated was lived out not in feelings of sweet, heart-fluttering romance but in screaming, tortured agony. Jesus didn't feel good on the cross. But it was love—real love, the commitment kind of love—that kept him there.

Jesus stayed.

And in doing so, he modeled the kind of love that really sustains a marriage—and ultimately fills it with plenty of romance too.

Marriage is about staying when we feel like going—because we have a mission that's more significant than our feelings.

Marriage is about more than making each other feel good. It's about a shared mission that gives life powerful meaning and purpose.

Marriage is not an end in itself. It's not about finding a nice person to have kids with and buying a nice house and a nice car so you can live a nice life until you're ready for a nice retirement. Does that really sound to you like the life the real God would intend for you to live? Marriage is about God's linking you up with a mission partner for a life that matters. It may be mostly happy or mostly sad, mostly rich or mostly poor, mostly healthy or mostly sick. But none of those things is the heart of it.

The heart of marriage is mission. God has a mission partner for you who will complete what is missing in you so that together you can live a life that really counts. And when life draws to a close, you'll be able to say, "Now that was a life!"

Your marriage must be missional.

2. Really Love Your Children

Well, that sounds easy.

But it's not really.

What does it mean to love our children? Does loving our children mean enjoying them like we enjoy watching a new puppy play? That's a lot of fun, but shouldn't love be deeper than that? That kind of love is all about the way our children make us feel. It's actually the height of self-centeredness. Real love, for parents, is the commitment to do everything we can, to give our lives for the privilege of shaping our children for their own mission.

I believe our children most need two things that we often give them the least. First, they need parents who love God with all their heart, soul, mind, and strength. That's rare, yet when it actually happens, it becomes a powerful force in their lives. This kind of love compels parents to make the hard choices, the big sacrifices, the wise decisions that lead their children to believe that God must be real—and is worth following. Second, they need parents who will give them away. We often spend our whole lives trying to keep our children. We want to keep them close by and protect them from anything risky. We want them to be near us as much as they can. We shelter them and pamper them and solve their problems for them. And in doing so, we never really entrust them to God.

But they're not ours!

If we believe that God is real, then we'll also believe that he loves our kids more than we do. So our ultimate goal, the height of love for our children, is to give them to him. If we believe God is real, we as parents must live as though he has *loaned* our children to us. Our ultimate goal is not to prepare them to be always safe and near us. Instead, we should be preparing them to risk everything to follow Jesus no matter where he may take them. For our family, that has meant doing things like taking our children on Third World mission trips at a very young age. It has meant moving our son across the country when he didn't want to go because we knew it was God's call. It has meant allowing our daughters to go and live in risky places that scared us to death but that fleshed out what we have taught them—that following Jesus is worth any and every risk. That the best place to be—the only place to be, but not necessarily the safe place to be—is with Jesus, wherever he summons them to go.

Parenting is not safe. We can't always protect our children. We might even lose them. God could choose to take them from us. We are not promised that we'll see our children live long lives. If you really want to know whether you believe God is real, ask yourself this question:

Will you trust him even if he takes your child from you?

Many times in my years of ministry, I've watched parents face the crushing blow of losing a child. Some of those times have provided for me the clearest ongoing evidence that God is, indeed, real. Parents who have lost children have taught me that

God is real in a way that's so powerful that he can transform even the most agonizing grief into joy. I have yet to find anything in the natural world that can do that.

Randy and Cherice Cottrell are among those parents who have shown me—and many others—the real God through the loss of their child.

I sat weeping with them in their home. Their precious baby, Colton, had died suddenly from SIDS. They were devastated. I could say nothing to fix it or to heal their shattered hearts. I told them one thing that I have come to believe because I have seen it so many times. Every time I say it, it sounds hollow. It sounds wrong. Because it *is* wrong . . . without the intervention of a supernatural God.

I told them that God would not waste their pain. That at some point, in some way, they would see it—that God would redeem their pain.

The months and weeks passed, and life moved on. But the real God was working in the Cottrells' life. One day, after a worship service, Cherice approached me while I was talking with people in our reception area. The only way I can describe her in that moment is aglow. She was aglow with the Spirit of God, emanating supernatural joy. She said, "Pastor, you were right. God has not wasted our pain." And then she said something so amazing that I'll never forget it: "I've come to the place that if I could take Colton back, I would not. I trust God so much that I would not change his plan." People were standing around, listening. I said to them, "Listen to this woman. If you came to this reception area to talk to me about a relationship with God, this is what it looks like. This is how powerfully God can work in you."

It was an amazing moment.

Cherice recently sent me this email:

For four months I have searched for the purpose in the loss of our precious baby. God created me and knows my personality: I am a doer, a fixer, an administrator, a problem solver. . . . I kept receiving God's consistent word to me: "Share what I have been to you through the darkest time of your life. Tell people that I am real, and tell them that I love them." My response was a somewhat bewildered, "That's it? That's all?" and God told me, "What could be more important?"

My days are mostly good and filled with an extraordinary peace. . . . Occasionally I have a very dark period of grief, but God is always with me. I never feel alone. . . . I feel crippled on the days when I focus on myself and try to get past that as quickly as possible. I ask God, "What do you have for me to do today?" and it helps me feel better.

My prayer life has been transformed! God has ignited in me the fiery passion for his word that I prayed for right before Colt died. Since we have experienced this tragedy, I truly know that God is real, and now I can't get close enough to him. . . . It stuns me that the God who created this universe and everything in it is so personal! He created me and loves me intimately! God is never away unless we push him.

God is never away unless we push him. I love that. And did you notice that in her pain and in her trust in God, she emphasized that she has found him to be real? As we raise our children, we need a God who is real. And we need to be parents who will love our kids enough to radically trust in God—the real God—even when it comes to their lives and their future.

Parenting is about more than enjoying your children.

Parenting is about forging a team with a purpose bigger than ourselves.

Parenting is about looking at the others around your dinner table and knowing that God brought you together for that very purpose.

Don't be so foolish as to think that other forces aren't battling to lead your children in a different direction. I've mentioned how much I enjoy spending time with atheists, but not everything about atheists is friendly and benign. Some have designs on your kids. Almost all of the "new atheists" who are writing bestselling books are pushing for a strategy to reeducate our children away from the "archaic" religious doctrines we've taught them. Some of what they propose is just scary. Richard Dawkins wrote: "How much do we regard children as being the property of their parents? It's one thing to say people should be free to believe whatever they like, but should they be free to impose their beliefs on their children? Is there something to be said for society stepping in?"[5]

Wow.

He's proposing the elimination of parents' rights to teach their children. He is not alone in this. And guess who will choose the "intellectually correct paths" that are to be taught to our children? Dawkins, of course, and those who share his nonbelief. Author Dinesh D'Souza wrote: "It seems that atheists are not content with committing cultural suicide—they want to take your children with them. The atheist strategy can be described this way: let the religious people breed them, and we will educate them to despise their parents' beliefs."[6]

This sort of blatant assault on our children demands that we have a solid defense. Parents who show their children the real God—who live out the passion of knowing him—guard against losing their children to destructive teachings like these. Children who live out family life on a mission with the real God will not easily trade that in for anything this world has to offer.

3. Embrace the Eternal Nature of Your Family's Adventure

Not to be depressing, but have you ever thought about the fact that one day no one will remember you? I've spent some time lately looking at our family tree. Names like Ransome Avant and Thomas Avent—people who mattered. They had lives like mine, children like mine. These people are important to me: I wouldn't be here without them.

But I never knew them. I never knew anyone who knew them. I know nothing about them except their names. Every memory of them is gone. One day my grandchildren's children's children's children will not know anyone who ever knew me. So if we live as though God doesn't really matter, then nothing really matters to our family. Because all of it will be gone and forgotten one day.

But there's a better way to live. It's a way that can infuse your family life with a sense of adventure that will last for eternity. Your family can actually believe what God says: that we are living for another world. Everything you are about as a family will have an impact and be remembered a trillion years from now—not here, but in the world that is really home. Your family needs an eternal focus.

What is your family mission? What are you doing to impact others for eternity? When is the last time you had someone in your home who didn't know Jesus—to model for him or her what real life following the real God looks like?

I love the question Mark Batterson asks in his wonderful book *In a Pit with a Lion on a Snowy Day*: *"Are you living your life in a way that is worth telling stories about?"*[7] That's the adventure your family is made for. If you live like that, when the time for the family reunion comes, spiritual passion and adventure will abound—even with weird Uncle Fred.

As you evaluate your own family, ask yourself these questions: What's the evidence in our family that we actually believe in God? How are we living differently from families who are just wandering through this world as though God were not real?

If God is real, he has to make a difference. And he does. Our family has seen it.

My wife's, Donna's, dad, Don Duniven, was not a good father. I'll let Donna tell you a little about that.

My first vivid memory of my dad was on a Sunday morning in church, when I was five, and he whispered in my ear, "Do you want to go talk to the pastor?" Tears were streaming down my face, and I remember wanting desperately to know this Jesus that the pastor was talking about.

I nodded yes through sobs, and my dad picked me up in strong arms and carried me to the front of the church. After talking to the pastor that day, I prayed to ask Jesus to come into my heart. Walking out of the church, I looked up at my dad and felt very sad for him. Even at that young age, I knew that my daddy didn't know Jesus—he just went to church.

Our family played the church game very well, but we didn't talk about God at our house. God was strictly for Sundays. The game ended abruptly when I was sixteen. One day my dad announced that we were having a family meeting. We'd never before had any sort of family meeting—much less family devotions or prayer times.

My sister and I took our appointed places on the gold velvet couch in the formal living room. My mom sat stiffly on the piano bench, Dad on the gold wingback chair.

"Girls," Dad said, "I want to talk to you about something—something that will change your lives. I love you, and this doesn't have anything to do with you. But your mom and I are getting a divorce."

I don't remember what was said after that—the room just seemed to spin out of control, and at that moment my whole life changed. Dad was right about that. I went from living with my whole family in a beautiful two-story suburban home to living in a two-bedroom apartment, with just Mom, next to the high school I attended. My sister lived with Dad and his new wife.

Dad wasn't really a part of my life after that—he showed up occasionally with his new wife—and in the span of twenty years he had three more wives. He ended up living in the same area we lived in for a few years, but he rarely made it to a birthday party—or even remembered birthdays. Or he would say he'd be there but not show up.

I never understood Donna's dad. How could he be so absent from her life? And from the lives of our children?

I knew this deeply affected Donna. When we married, I observed something strange and sad. I'm a night owl and like to study late, but my wife is asleep by ten. So I pray with her when she goes to bed and then join her later. But when I'd open the door to enter the room, she'd say in her sleep, "Daddy? Daddy?" I'd wake her up, but she never remembered it. That just made me madder at Don for the emotional pain he caused my sweet wife. But Donna never gave up on her daddy. She prayed for him and always believed God—that one day he would change her father.

One February day in 1996, Don called my wife to talk. He told her that he was in Atlanta for a business meeting. Donna told him that, coincidentally, I was in Atlanta speaking. Don said, "I'll go hear him preach." Donna was ecstatic. Her dad had never heard me preach.

I was just angry. I knew he wouldn't come. He would let her down again. Donna rebuked me and told me to act as though I had some semblance of faith and pray with her.

When I walked out onto the platform to preach that night, I couldn't believe my eyes. There, in the back row, was Don Duniven.

I knew that Donna had called many people and asked them to pray. I knew that a real spiritual battle was raging in the soul of this troubled man. I knew that our real God was there, reaching out to Don. And when I finished preaching, Don Duniven reached back. I watched him begin to shake, visibly weeping, and then he stumbled down the aisle. I walked down to meet him right in the middle of the church. He fell into my arms and choked out these words: "I've ruined my life and hurt all those I love. Can God ever forgive me?"

In those moments, the real God entered Don's life. I was overwhelmed. No one in the church knew what was going on until I told them Don's story. God moved in that place, and life after life was touched and transformed that night. We were there a long time, but no one seemed to mind.

Finally the service came to an end, and Don and I went out to eat. We sat together and talked for hours. He fielded all the questions about my wife as a child that I'd never been able to ask. That night Don Duniven became my friend as well as my brother. We even shared the gospel with the waitress. I'm still amazed at that night, even now.

When I finally got back to my hotel room after midnight, I called Donna. I hardly knew what to say. Barely halfway into the first ring, she answered. She'd been sitting there holding the phone. "Donna," I said, "I don't know how to tell you this, but you have a new daddy."

"Don't tease me," she said.

"I wouldn't tease you about this. Your dad met Jesus in front of the whole church tonight." She dropped the phone. Let her tell you what happened next.

I remember that phone call as though it were yesterday.

I had dozed off holding the phone, waiting for John to call.

As soon as I heard, "Donna, you have a new daddy!" My heart felt as if it were going to explode.

I had prayed so long for my dad. I knew he was miserable—he had just been asked to retire, his marriage was in trouble—again—and he was close to bankruptcy.

I had begged God for his salvation. . . . Honestly, as much as he had hurt me, I still loved him, and the thought of him spending eternity apart from Christ—apart from me—was unbearable. I actually began praying for his salvation when I was five years old—the day, walking out of church, when I looked up into his face and knew he didn't know the Jesus I had just embraced.

I did drop the phone. I ran to each of my children's rooms—woke them up out of a sound sleep as I knocked on their doors and began yelling, "Grandpa got saved!" "Grandpa accepted Christ!"

Poor babies—Trey, age five; Amy, age eight; and Christi, age eleven. They had to know—they had to understand that God had answered our prayers! They had to know that the God we talked about at home—the God we prayed to and sang to and served—was real!

Don Duniven became a new man: a real dad to Donna, a real granddaddy to our children. The kids adored him. He would drive from Oklahoma to Atlanta to see Christi sing and act, and he screamed himself hoarse at Trey's football games. When Amy won the state championship in volleyball, I don't think he could speak for a week!

And from that first night that God gave Donna a new dad, she has never again called out for him in the dark of night. Her heart and spirit no longer felt the need to call for him. Her daddy had come home.

Ten wonderful years went by before the shocking call came that Don had died in his sleep. We were devastated yet comforted by the joy of answered prayer, of a dear family member's transformed life. Here's Donna's account:

Dad went to live with Jesus on November 7, 2005. The coroner said he died of a massive heart attack in his sleep.

When I walked into his apartment a few days later, one thing was very clear: Jesus had become central in this man's life—and so had his family. Lying next to his bed was his Bible; his reading glasses were on top of it, along with some other Christian growth books we had given him. Pictures of my sister and me and the grandchildren were everywhere. Taped to his computer screen and the inside of his checkbook was this verse: "Oh, that you would bless me and enlarge my territory! Let your hand be with me, and keep me from harm so that I will be free from pain" (1 Chronicles 4:10). My dad had obviously been praying this verse for himself. Was God real? Did God answer that prayer?

As I sat with my family in the front of the chapel for his funeral, about sixty young men came in and sat together as a group. These were the young men my dad had taught at school—he taught them how to work on farm equipment or construction equipment. When the service was over and they filed by to pay their respects, I heard over and over these words: "You dad was a great man. He was like a father to me!"

It matters when one life is changed. It matters when a family is changed and healed. And it matters that God is real and is the Changer and the Healer. If you believe that, then live it out in your own family. If you face a situation in your family that seems impossible, trust the real God. He loves your family more than you do—even those members who don't love him back. Nothing will cause you to believe he is real more than to see him at work in your family . . . and then to see him use your family to touch and change someone else. If he could do that in and through Don Duniven, he can do it through anyone.

Don't miss a minute of your eternal adventure together. The God on whom we have staked everything is able to do more in you and through you and your family than you can dream. Believe him.

5

If God Were Real ...
the Church Would Be Full of Addicts

Addicts have defected from the living God.
Instead of worshipping in the temple of the Lord,
they perform addictive rituals that give them more
perceived power, pleasure, or identity.
They see in their addiction a form of magic.
Edward T. Welch, *Addictions*

JUST LEFT THE kitchen. I've done it again. I knew I would do it before I even went into the kitchen.

I ate the entire container of Blue Bell Homemade Vanilla ice cream.

Well, someone had already eaten a little, but I cleaned out enough to serve about twenty people. Even poured raspberry sauce all over it as if half a million calories and ten thousand carbs were not enough. And though I should have felt guilty as I ate it, I really didn't. It was just too good. I stuffed it in, smiling the whole time. Only when the last bit was gone and the spoon licked clean did the guilt and shame begin to set in.

Why did I do that? I'm convinced I'm addicted to the stuff. Is there a twelve-step program for ice-cream-aholics? *Merriam-*

Webster's Collegiate Dictionary describes addiction as "persistent compulsive use of a substance known by the user to be harmful." For me, that's ice cream. I know it's not good for me. Diabetes runs in my family, and my doctor has told me that I'm a prime candidate for it if I don't keep my weight under control. So I run. A lot. And then I defeat the purpose by going on an all-out ice-cream binge. This isn't my first offense. I've done this over and over again. When the Blue Bell Homemade Vanilla ice cream is in the freezer, it's as if I can hear it calling to me—quietly at first, and then louder and louder until the voice is practically screaming in my head: "Eat me! Enjoy me! You need me!"

Now, I know that in the arena of addictions, mine would be considered pretty mild and relatively harmless. But it still illustrates a stunning contradiction in me. I say that I believe in God. I claim to believe that he has revealed himself through the Scriptures—that the words of the Bible were breathed by the Creator himself. And his Word tells me: "Do you not know that your body is a temple of the Holy Spirit, who is in you, whom you have received from God? You are not your own; you were bought at a price. Therefore honor God with your body" (1 Corinthians 6:19–20). So why do I dishonor God by deliberately doing something that will damage my body? Why do I eat all the ice cream?

Think about what I did in light of that passage:

- It tells me that as a Christ follower, the Holy Spirit is in me. Yet I tried to push him out with gallons of ice cream.
- It says that I don't belong to myself. That implies that I stole myself away from my rightful Lord so I could do what I wanted, contrary to his command.

- The command to honor God with my body is clear. But I elevated myself to God's place when I chose to honor myself—as well as the Blue Bell Ice Cream company and the manufacturers of the bigger pants I'll have to buy.

My body is the temple of the Lord—designed as a vessel of worship. But I obeyed the call of another master. I abandoned obedience to God's call for moderation and obeyed my own urge for ice cream—in massive, unhealthy quantities. Worst of all, I became an idolater, intensely longing for something not worthy of such affection. With God right there with me, I openly worshiped another. I bowed down to my idols of pleasure and indulgence with spoon in hand. My idolatry is not much different from what we read about in the Bible. It's just that my golden calf is vanilla flavored.

All addicts do that—value something inferior more than they value God. Addiction is a powerfully destructive force in our communities—and yes, even in our churches. "Only 5 percent of the [drug and alcohol] addicts in America live on skid row," according to Nelson Price. "Many attend our churches regularly. Addicts are good actors and actresses, and our congregations are filled with actors and actresses."[1] So the church is full of addicts—some addicted to drugs, alcohol, or other destructive substances. Many more are addicted to habits that, while not illegal, are disobedient to God and displace God from the position of honor and priority that rightfully belongs to him alone.

I believe the fundamental causes of addiction are unbelief and idolatry. If I really believed what the Bible says about God and about my own body, I would never take the first step down the road to addiction. But it's much easier to seek those things I can see and feel and touch and taste than it is to seek God. Human nature, like water, runs downhill. I'm drawn to things that indulge my love of pleasure and love of myself. And once I experience them, it's easy to start putting them at the center of my life, to have them on my mind all the time, to think about the next time I can experience them and how to get more. And so I become a worshiper of something other than God. I believe in the pleasure of addiction more than in the truth of God. My addiction is my god, my love. Like Tolkien's Gollum, I have found "my precious."

The Problem of Addiction

Northeast Louisiana, where I live, is beautiful. I love it here. Our Ouachita River is one of the most beautiful stretches of river in America. We have wonderful lakes and forests full of wildlife. We have fabulous food, great athletic teams, and the best people on earth.

But we also have enormous problems: economic, racial, educational, and family challenges. The church I pastor has a vision to see our community transformed. Everyone here recognizes the complexity of accomplishing such transformation. I've been asking leaders across our area what they consider to be our biggest challenge. I asked our mayors, the district attorney, the sheriff, the police chief, the marshal, and a lot of others. I got the same answer from virtually everyone.

Drug abuse is our number one problem. It's destroying our families, killing our children, wrecking our economy, and creating poverty. Almost every bad thing in our community has some link to the drug problem. In my first six months here, I buried two young men who died from drug overdoses. Two promising young lives were over far too soon because of this poison.

Shouldn't it be amazing to us that anyone would choose that first encounter with drugs in the first place? After all, could there be anyone in America who does not know that this stuff will kill you? I don't think a lack of education about drugs is our problem. We watch film and TV stars who seem to have everything anyone could want descend into a hell of their own making. We watched what felt like endless media coverage of the drug-related deaths of Anna Nicole Smith and Heath Ledger. We've seen Britney Spears and Lindsay Lohan, just a few years past childhood, come apart before our eyes. We hear the stories in every community and every school. And yet many people still pursue the pleasure of drugs as if, somehow, they'll be the exception—the only ones who escape the misery and death that are the price of addiction.

For those who escape the lure of actual drugs, something else will become their virtual drug. Eating disorders have become epidemic. Just a few weeks ago, in our own church, a woman came to the front for prayer. She weighed something like sixty pounds. The room got quiet. I told our people that because of this woman's eating disorder, she would soon die. We cried out to God on her behalf, and people gave the money needed to get her into an intensive in-house treatment center. It's ironic that while some like me are addicted to food—like ice cream—others are addicted to not eating—ice cream, or anything else.

Sexual addictions are also increasingly rampant. With easy access to Internet porn, many of our children become addicts from the beginning of puberty. And the effect of such degrading sexual addictions on the future of this generation is terrifying. Studies just released show that fully 25 percent of teen girls now have a sexually transmitted disease. And if you count only those who have already had sex, the number almost doubles. Nearly half of those girls have sexually transmitted diseases.[2]

The pull of sexual addiction is so strong that even presidents and governors trade integrity and careers for the pleasure. I watched with the rest of America, stunned, as Governor Eliot Spitzer of New York, a man many believed would one day be president of the United States, resigned after being caught up in a prostitution ring. Every reporter on television was asking how in the world Spitzer thought he could avoid being caught. He was the governor of New York! But addictions aren't about thinking. They're about worshiping. All thought is secondary to the thrill of the worship experience, the preeminence of the idol. And then, no sooner had David Paterson, the new governor, been sworn into office when he admitted that both he and his wife had also had extramarital affairs. What a mess we're in!

That seems much worse than my eating all the ice cream. Still, it's not all that different. We're an addicted culture, even within the church. We always will be—until we fully make up our minds that God is real. If he is, and if he's all the Bible says he is, then clearly we don't need drugs. We don't need sexual sin. We don't need too much food or to starve ourselves. We just need him.

But we're not there yet. I'm not there yet. I believe in God. I love God. But I still love my idols just a little too much to live like God is real all the time.

The Pattern of Untransformed Lives

Why is the gospel not transforming more lives? That's the question my brother posed the other day. We spent quite a while discussing that problem. My brother Mike is a physician, saving the lives of children every day, and a key leader in a large church. We have very different lives but puzzle over the same strange truth that both of us see around us all the time: most people's lives don't seem to be fundamentally changed by the gospel.

Statistics seem to bear this out. Studies by George Barna, George Gallup, and others show little difference in the way Christians live when compared with those who don't believe in our God. Divorce rates are about the same. Addictions are about the same. How can this be? I believe it all comes down to unbelief. If we truly believed, our lives would be transformed. Our untransformed lives demonstrate a pattern of unbelief that leaves us struggling, ineffective for God, and powerless. What is this pattern of unbelief that dooms us to live untransformed lives?

We Don't Believe in God's Mission

The first followers of Christ believed in his mission: to be a transformational force in the kingdom of God and to make sure everyone has the chance to be in that kingdom. They were willing to die for it. One might almost say they were addicted to accomplishing that mission. They had seen the risen Christ for themselves. Following him was their passion and joy. They needed nothing else. Often they had nothing else. Nothing but pain, persecution, and poverty. But when they helped advance God's mission, they experienced a high greater than any drug can offer.

Acts 13 shows us a great example. Paul and Barnabas had come to Pisidian Antioch to preach, and "almost the whole city gathered to hear the word of the Lord" (v. 44). The leaders of the city became so angry that they ran Paul and Barnabas completely out of the region. Yet "the disciples were filled with joy and with the Holy Spirit" (v. 52).

Why were they so happy? Because "the word of the Lord spread through the whole region" (v. 49). Their mission was not to be happy, to win fame or security, or to seek personal pleasure. Their mission was the mission of God. They believed in him enough to trust that if their lives advanced his mission, they would be fulfilled beyond anything the world could give them. Today, as then, those who really believe in God are willing to lay down their lives to pursue his mission—because nothing in their lives is more real or more important.

We've come a long way from that in the church today. We're so internally focused that, as I've already said, it's highly questionable whether we even have the same mission as the New Testament church anymore—whether we *are* the New Testament church anymore. When we are given over to a mission, our lives find a central focus. Without that mission and focus, we are more easily drawn to self and the self-focus that leads to bondage. If we really believed in the mission of God, the urgency of what is at stake would compel us to turn from the idols of our addictions.

We Don't Believe in God's Discipline

The Bible is full of the stories of God's discipline of his children. Sometimes that discipline seems mild and his patience unending. But other times it's clear that God's discipline is serious business.

- For the sin of rebellion, the people of Israel wandered forty years and died in the wilderness.
- For disobeying God, Saul lost his kingdom and then his life.
- For adultery and murder, David lost his child.

David spoke about God's discipline in Psalm 39: "You rebuke and discipline men for their sin; you consume their wealth like a moth—each man is but a breath" (v. 11).

One of the clearest signs of our lack of belief in God is that we don't seem to fear or even have any real concern about coming under his discipline when we have given ourselves over to idols, to the worship of the false gods of our lusts and desires. The apostle Paul urged, "My dear friends, flee from idolatry. I speak to sensible people" (1 Corinthians 10:14–15). But we are not sensible people anymore. Our senses have been dulled by the strange pull of the world, which has become more precious to us than God himself.

God has given us one life to live, one chance to breathe this air, one amazing opportunity to be a steward of his creation and an ambassador of the Creator. If God is real, and what he says is true, should we not fear the consequences if we throw all that away for a moment of selfish pleasure? Sadly, we seem to fear the loss of our pleasure far more than we fear the wrath of God, whose very existence we apparently doubt.

We Don't Believe in God's Goodness

Addicts are after what is good—what feels so good to them that they would risk anything for it. How would it change our lives and our addictions if we believed that ultimate goodness resided in the nature of God? If we believed that Jesus died to take away all that wrecks our lives and that he rose to give us full life that starts here and never ends, wouldn't we believe that nothing in this world is better for us, more fulfilling for us, than the goodness of God? "Taste and see that the LORD is good; blessed is the man who takes refuge in him" (Psalm 34:8). For most Christians, the taste of the Lord's goodness seems to have faded from our memories.

And that seems strange in light of the proliferation of feel-good books and TV preachers in America. It seems there's a new book on the shelves every week with some title like *Living the Good Life with God.* So why, if we snatch up these books the way sales records say we do, and if we're filling up churches that make us feel good . . . do we not seem to feel good? Why is "the good life with God" not enough, and more and more Christians worship the same addictive idols as non-Christians?

Maybe the problem is that we've made "the good life with God" another idol, when only the experience of God himself, for his sake and not ours, will really satisfy us.

Instead of the real God, we find our refuge in the gods we make for ourselves. But although the taste of these idolatrous gods is sweet at first, it soon becomes as bitter as poison. Still we feed on them. And feed we will until we finally really believe that what we'll find in God is better than anything we can find anywhere else. Only then will we hunger for God, tasting and seeing God's goodness in our own lives.

When we believe in God's mission, making God's desire to see people come to him our own; when we believe in God's discipline—that we face dire consequences when we fail to put God above all else; and when we believe in God's goodness—and want what he offers us more than any temporary pleasure or self-indulgence; only then will our lives be transformed and will we be freed from our addictions.

So how do we do this? How do we move away from the worship of our addictions into the authentic worship of God in a way that takes him seriously—as if he were real? If we really believed that God is real, what would we do?

We'd start by pursuing holiness.

The Pursuit of Holiness

"God did not call us to be impure, but to live a holy life" (1 Thessalonians 4:7). It seems that a holy life would be the opposite of an addicted life. But the word *holy* has gotten a bad rap lately. Think about it. How many people would like to be known as holy? It sounds like someone who thinks he's better than everyone else or someone who can't relate to the real world. But that's far from the true meaning of the word *holy*. To be holy means to be set apart for God's purpose! Now, if God is real and loves us desperately, if Jesus died and rose to give us life, and if all the rest that we say we believe about God is true, why wouldn't everyone want to be set apart for his purpose?

When I was a young follower of Christ, I heard a lot about holiness. I also read what great Christ followers of the past had written about holiness. It seemed that the very heart of the Christian faith was the pursuit of holiness. But I don't hear much about holiness anymore. Not in the traditional church. I hear rants about the favorite sin we want to bash that day, but that has little to do with holiness. And I don't hear about it in the contemporary church either. In fact, it seems to me that the goal of some in the emerging church (which I largely support, by the way) is to see how much we can imitate those who *don't* follow Christ. How much can we get away with in order to be hip? How dirty can we talk? How much can we drink? How many nudity-filled movies can we brag about seeing?

Maybe Christians of all stripes have lost something really precious. And maybe that loss, the loss of holiness, has made us tragically vulnerable to the power of our addictions.

I don't consider myself holy. I'm pretty sad about that. I think I'm way too influenced by the world I live in. I read great writers like A. W. Tozer, who said, "We are called to an everlasting preoccupation with God,"[3] but I don't often feel preoccupied with God. I do want to be holy, however. I want the passion for holiness that seems to have marked authentic followers of Christ in every era. In that passion I think we may find a key to freedom from bondage.

It seems to me that in life, everyone will be "set apart" for something. We'll all give ourselves to something or someone. We seem made to do it—to seek some great pleasure, some all-consuming adventure that takes us out of the mundane, that adds joy and mystery to our existence. For too many people, that ends up being a substance, sex, or some other such thing. But what if we believed in God enough to make pursuing him our adventure, our great pleasure, our addiction?

I want that to be my pursuit.

I really do. Today—or at least right now. But I know that tomorrow, or maybe even later today, other adventures will call to me. Other things for which I can choose to be set apart. But I have seen the results of choosing all those other things many, many times.

I think I'll pursue God.

I think I'll pursue holiness.

Doesn't that really offer us the best hope? Our only real chance to find the essence of what we seek so futilely in our addictions? Saint Augustine of Hippo traded in his addictions for that pursuit. He expressed it like this:

> I came to love you late, O Beauty so ancient and new; I came to love you late. You were within me and I was outside, where I rushed about wildly searching for You like some monster loose in Your beautiful world. You were with me, but I was not with You. You called me, You shouted to me, You wrapped me in Your splendor, You sent my blindness reeling. You gave out such a delightful fragrance, and I drew it in and came breathing hard after You. I tasted and it made me hunger and thirst; You touched me, and I burned to know Your peace.[4]

Oh, it's so late, and I've wasted so much time! But I long for the end of that pursuit Augustine talked about. I believe as I pursue holiness, as I pursue God, I will find that my path leads to the living God and away from that which would enslave me. Yes, when we truly live as though God is real and pursue holiness, the church will be full of addicts: people addicted to God. Then what transformation we'd see in our lives, our churches, our communities, and our world! Such a community of believers would turn the world upside down for God—just as a similar community of believers did two thousand years ago.

When my brother asked me why I thought the gospel transforms so few lives today, my first idea was that the answer is pretty simple: we don't live in the kind of community the gospel is meant to transform.

It's pretty clear in the New Testament that the gospel was not a gift to an individual. Sure, the good news of Jesus transforms individuals; but in the New Testament, that happened in a tight-knit, relational family: "All the believers were together and had everything in common. Selling their possessions and goods, they gave to anyone as he had need. Every day they continued to meet together in the temple courts. They broke bread in their homes and ate together with glad and sincere hearts" (Acts 2:44–46).

That passage features a lot of togetherness. They gathered together, shared together, worshiped together, ate together, went to one another's homes, and rejoiced together. Most Christians today sit *among* a bunch of people—not *with* them—in rows, looking at the backs of heads, in a vast room once a week at best . . . and then wonder why the gospel doesn't change their lives!

We're designed to be a *family*—a dynamic organism led by the Spirit of God—knowing, loving, and helping one another. Perhaps the greatest thing a church could do to help its members break free from bondage is to do anything it takes to transform Sunday-school classes and Bible studies into New Testament communities of love, vulnerability, compassion, and power. That's how the gospel was meant to transform us. If the pursuit of holiness is what will break our bondage, then how much better if we make that pursuit together?

The Power of Transformation

God can transform our lives—whether we're addicted to popularity, attention, adrenaline rushes, the New Orleans Saints, or ice cream. God has the power to deliver us from our addictions. No other person or thing or program can ever really fill the empty spot deep within us that we so desperately try to fill. No matter what our temptation, no matter what our need, God is enough. God tells us, "I am your shield, your very great reward" (Genesis 15:1). I know this is true. In fact, God has shown me the truth of this so many times that I can't even count them.

God is enough!

I know this. He's all the reward I need. He's the source of my life, he fills me with every good thing. He is enough . . . but there's ice cream in the freezer again. Company is coming, and in the time I've been writing this chapter, my wife bought some more Blue Bell. And I still feel like I need it all.

I guess I'll have to decide what I really worship. If I worshiped my way into addictions, I will have to worship my way out. I'll have to actually try living as though God is enough; not just talking about it but actually living it out for an extended period of time. Time enough for him to show me—again—that he really is all I need.

I think you will have to do this too—if you believe God is real.

They say you can change major life patterns in forty days. What if you gave this a shot—to let God be your addiction for the next forty days? To pursue him the way you pursue other things for pleasure. If he doesn't show himself to be real, you can always go back to all that other stuff you've been pursuing. But if you find what you've been missing in God, well, then you've found life.

As I write this, it's Easter Sunday—the first Easter with my new family, the wonderful people of First Baptist Church of

West Monroe, Louisiana. We had five services this weekend, and I'm still amazed by the experience. It was the real deal today. It was not a show, and people could sense it. We were in the presence of the risen Christ. After one of the services, I spoke with a prominent businessman in our church. Actually he has only been in our church for a few weeks. During that time he met the real God and has begun a journey away from his years-long addiction to drugs. He can't stop telling everyone what Jesus has done for him.

Another young man in bondage to drugs began his journey to freedom today as he came face-to-face with the Resurrected One and surrendered his addiction to him.

These people are far from alone. Across the sea of thousands of faces, I saw one after another who has been set free.

Like Keith and Shaundra. You won't find any better people in our church than these two. But not too many years ago, Shaundra was completely addicted to alcohol, hiding bottles in her purse, even drinking while picking up her kids from school. "My marriage was also beginning to fall apart," she says. "I was extremely prideful and selfish. This time of my life was truly a living hell. Keith moved out, into an apartment. At my lowest point, I remember sitting on my bed, and I thought about the shotgun in the closet."

But the real God set her free.

Here's how Shaundra explains it:

All I can say is, I was miraculously and instantaneously healed. I woke up one morning and knew I wasn't going to drink again. God even took away all desire for alcohol. For months, maybe years, I thanked God every single day for keeping me sober. Then one day I realized that I hadn't thanked him in a few days, and I realized I hadn't even thought of alcohol in that time! God took a miserable, selfish drunk and turned me into a woman absolutely in love with and on fire for my Jesus. He took a seriously troubled marriage and transformed it into a relationship with amazing love. To this day, I have not had one desire to drink alcohol. He really, really can do more than we can possibly imagine. My entire life is a walking miracle.

I also saw Jonathan in that crowd. He'd been diagnosed as a teen with an eating disorder and had sought both medical and psychological help. He was in bondage to something that threatened his very life.

But the real God set him free.

Jonathan says, "I began to earnestly pray and meditate on God's Word. After many months, I was free! God delivered me from the bondage of that sickness and made me whole again." Today Jonathan is a newlywed and just started seminary to prepare for ministry.

I saw Kevin, sitting with his fiancée. We will be commissioning Kevin as a missionary soon—to the prison where he will be spending six months. His drug case has been in the courts for years, and during this time he has become a faithful part of our church. Kevin says:

My addiction took me down a long, dark road full of misery, loneliness, and immorality. It eventually led to my being arrested. After my arrest, I spent a week in jail. My first night in the cell, I dropped to my knees, cried for hours, and turned everything over to the Lord. I asked him for forgiveness and strength to change my life. From that moment forward, the power of my addiction disappeared, and my heart was filled with an immense feeling of love and joy. I now have sight of my purpose in life. I live for God and want to take my experience to as many others as I can to help them see his greatness. Even though I have to go back to jail, I know God has a plan for me and wants to use me to share that he can make all bad things right, and if we come to him, the darkness is erased and filled with brightness.

The real God has set him free, a freedom even prison walls can't take away.

Those are just a few of the stories of the people I saw before me on this Easter Sunday, people who are my friends and my family. There are many, many more—here and all over the world.

If God is real, the church should be full of addicts—whose God-addicted lives will be testimonies of God's love and power to transform broken, hurting people into healing, joyful Christ followers. Our churches should be full of people who have finally found what they're searching for, what they're craving, in Christ.

Testimonies like theirs are some of those wonderful reasons why, though it seems that so much of the time we live as though God is not real, I know that he is. Because when we treat him like he's real, he shows himself to be so. And he does it over and over again, for all who will seek him.

And so, as I finish this chapter on this Easter Sunday night, I know I will rest well tonight, in joy and in freedom—and in the arms of the real God.

Before I go to bed, I think I will have some ice cream . . . but only a little.

6

If God Were Real . . .
We'd Live in a Messed-up World

The existence of evil is not so much an obstacle to faith in
God as proof of God's existence, a challenge to turn toward
that in which love triumphs over hatred, union over
division, and eternal life over death.
Nikolai Aleksandrovich Berdyaev

SOMETHING IS WRONG—REALLY wrong—with this world.

"Matt's dad killed himself," my son said to Donna and me yesterday as we stared at him in disbelief. Matt had recently visited with us. He's my son's friend and football teammate from the city where we used to live. His entire family and ours are friends.

This sad news came on the same day I'd ministered to a young church planter and friend whose brother, a pastor, had also just killed himself. And on the news tonight, a large group of young girls was rescued from a cult compound in Texas where it's alleged that some had been married off to older men and abused physically and sexually. Plus, four young people from a California youth group were killed in a car accident. All in a day. Just another day like every day in this world—where unbearable suffering and agony are inescapable facts of life.

How can God be real in a messed-up world like ours?

Sometimes I'm haunted by that thought. As a pastor, I've seen so much pain, helped bury so many people who died for what seem like senseless reasons, that I've had dark moments of doubt when I hear a foul voice whisper that I've believed a lie.

But not most of the time.

Most of the time I'm captivated by a truth that's easy to miss: *the world is exactly how we should expect it to be if the Bible is true.*

Let me share with you a brief story.

I was talking recently with a friend of mine who is an atheist. We talked about her concerns about Christianity, which are many. As is often the case, I find commonality with many atheists at this point because I agree with many of their concerns about the form of Christianity we have created. So we had a cordial and interesting conversation. Then I asked her about the issue of God's existence. I wanted to see inside her heart, learn what really caused her rejection of the God who is so real and personal to me. "In the deepest part of your heart," I asked her, "Why is it that you don't believe in God?"

I expected an answer formulated on an intellectual or scientific basis. She's a brilliant woman. But her answer surprised me. "I just don't feel like he's there," she said. We were quiet for a moment, and then she elaborated. "When I look at all the terrible suffering and pain in the world, I just feel in my heart that there couldn't be a God overseeing all this."

It was an honest, vulnerable answer. I was moved that she would share it so openly with me. She had spoken from her heart to me, and I wanted to do the same in return. I didn't want to give her a sterile, apologetic answer. I breathed a prayer that God would give me the right words to say. I don't know if I had ever said to anyone or even clearly thought out the answer I gave her. I said, "I understand. Sometimes I feel that way too. But it helps me to realize that the world in all its mess is just what it would be if God were real." I could tell she was genuinely intrigued by this. She didn't become a theist that day, but our conversation caused us both to think about these things more deeply. Think with me.

In his wonderful book *The Reason for God,* Timothy Keller says, "If the world is fallen, broken, and needs to be redeemed, that explains the violence and disorder we see."[1] In other words, the world is exactly how the Bible describes it. Romans 8:21 says that the whole earth is in "bondage to decay." It's not just we humans who groan and suffer because of the evil and destruction in this world. Verse 22 tells us that "the whole creation has been groaning." If the story of the fall of mankind in Genesis 3 is real, then we shouldn't be surprised at all that the world is wrecked. Rather, we should be amazed that by the grace and mercy of God any beauty, wonder, and goodness remain at all.

The world is full of great beauty, but it's marred. It's not whole. It's only a shadow of the perfect world God intends for us. We are fallen, and our world has fallen with us. Keller goes on to say, "Human beings are so integral to the fabric of things that when human beings turned from God, the entire warp and woof of the world unraveled. Disease, genetic disorders, famine, natural disasters, aging, and death itself are as much the result of sin as are oppression, war, crime, and violence."[2]

Neither the church nor the secular world seems to really get this. *Time* recently ran a feature with the cover title "What Makes Us Good/Evil?" in which it avoided any discussion about the possible effect of sin in the world. In *World* magazine Joel Belz wrote:

"In more than 3,000 words, the broad topic of 'religion' is never suggested. There's not a hint that anybody has ever talked about something called the 'Fall.' It's breathtaking, in fact, that *Time* could take on a cover story like 'What Makes Us Good/Evil?' and leave out so much that seems so basic."[3]

If we do leave the Fall out of the picture, then there seems no way to explain a loving God's existence in such an unloving place. But the church has not done much better in the way of explanation. As in much of what we do, we learn to leave the real God out of the picture. When we suffer or others suffer, we tend to just say, "It must have been God's will." But what if saying that is really just an excuse to keep us from having to answer the most important question the real God might want us to consider: what should we do about suffering?

We should be somewhat comforted to understand that our messed-up world is actually evidence of God's existence and the truth of his Word. But if we're not willing to do anything about it, then we're right back to our practical atheism. What difference does it make whether God is real?

Keller talks about the Hebrew concept of *shalom:*

It means absolute wholeness—full, harmonious, joyful, flourishing life.

The devastating loss of *shalom* through sin is described in Genesis 3. We are told that as soon as we determined to serve ourselves instead of God—as soon as we abandoned living for and enjoying God as our highest good—the entire created world became broken. . . . We have lost God's *shalom*—physically, spiritually, socially, psychologically, culturally. Things now fall apart.[4]

We know that only God can redeem the world. And if he is real, the entire story of the Fall and the coming of a Savior who will ultimately redeem this broken world shines the light of hope on our suffering and makes sense out of all our nonsense.

But we're still left to deal with a very big issue: what do we do now—while we're still living in this broken world?

Though we cannot reverse the Fall, is it possible that we as Christ followers can be the restorers of shalom? Is it possible that this is our whole purpose? If God is real, how would a real God want us to live in a fallen world?

Become Transformational Healers

One of the strongest rebukes to leaders in the Bible is found in the thirty-fourth chapter of Ezekiel. God says to the spiritual leaders of Israel, "You have not strengthened the weak or healed the sick or bound up the injured. You have not brought back the strays or searched for the lost. You have ruled them harshly and brutally" (Ezekiel 34:4). Since I'm a pastor, this passage has always made me uneasy. Could I be one of the shepherds the Lord rebukes? I think so. And I think I may have a lot of company.

If anything at all is clear in Scripture, it's that the followers of the living God have always been meant to be a force for healing and transformation. But we've become so crippled by our self-centered, inward-focused churches that we ourselves need healing. Hebrews 12:12–13 says: "Therefore, strengthen your feeble arms and weak knees. 'Make level paths for your feet,' so that the lame may not be disabled, but rather healed." I don't want to be a weak-kneed leader! I don't want people around me to be disabled when they could be whole. And it sure looks like people can be whole—and that there's something we can do to help make them so—if God is real.

A prominent teaching of Jesus in the New Testament is the concept of the kingdom of God. We can't really understand what Jesus says apart from understanding the kingdom. Jesus sometimes spoke of the kingdom in its final consummation at the end of time, but mostly he talked about the kingdom as present reality. He came to establish a new order, and he expects his followers to live in the realm of the kingdom and in the healing power of the King. "He sent them out to preach the kingdom of God and to heal the sick" (Luke 9:2).

I know there's a lot of controversy about healing today, and, frankly, I'm skeptical of television healers who seem mostly to "heal" their own bank accounts. Yet I believe God still heals people physically today. I've witnessed it. But I think we might see a lot more of the miraculous if we were first healed of our own selfishness and began to advance the kingdom of God. We might not all agree about physical healing, but surely we can agree that Jesus intended for his followers to heal the hurts of those around us as we are able. If we can help the poor rise out of their poverty, help an orphan find a family, help an addict to be free, then we must do it! This is how we as Christ followers help advance the kingdom of God.

The kingdom of God is doing just fine, by the way. It's advancing all over the world. In the farthest reaches of the earth you can find Christ followers touching people at their point of need, transforming broken lives, and giving the credit to Jesus and his kingdom at work. But in America we are so intent on building our own kingdoms that it's sometimes harder to see the kingdom of God at work here.

It's time for that to change.

In Matthew 11:12 Jesus said, "From the days of John the Baptist until now, the kingdom of heaven has been forcefully advancing, and forceful men lay hold of it." It's time for the church to lay hold of the transforming power of the kingdom of God. It's our spiritual birthright, and there's no reason we should let it pass us by. It's time for transformation and healing to become the talk of the town—*your* town. Until that happens, most unbelievers will keep seeing us as the people of the big mouth. Right now, if they happen to hear us talk about the kingdom or changing the world, it just scares them to death. They assume that the change means controlling them, defeating them, or even hurting them.

Our mission should be to heal the brokenness around us that the Lord gives us power to heal so that when the world hears us proclaiming the kingdom, they'll look around at the change and say, "Oh! So that's what they're talking about. We've never seen anything like that before." If the world began to say that, we'd know we were finally living like followers of Jesus. We'd be following his example when he walked the earth, healing the sick and hurting. "We have never seen anything like this!" they said when Jesus healed a paralyzed man (Mark 2:12). Yet what really amazed them was not just that he had healed the man but that he confronted religious legalism and forgave the man's sins. Jesus met the hurting man's real need: he healed not just his body but also his soul. He restored the man's shalom. And as he did it, he broke the back of the religious rules and hypocrisy that were keeping people from God in his day.

If those who don't believe in God are to have any hope of

coming to believe, it is vital that they see those of us who say we believe in God act like we do.

So how do we get started?

Become Ultimate Fighters

I'm a huge fan of the relatively new sport known as "ultimate fighting" or, more accurately, mixed martial arts. To me it's the ultimate blend of athleticism, skill, and combat. Anyone who knows anything at all about the sport knows that it's much more than two guys in a brawl trying to kill each other. The best ultimate fighters are highly trained in multiple disciplines. They may be skilled wrestlers and boxers, but they also may have black belts in other disciplines such as Brazilian Jiu-Jitsu, judo, karate, and Thai boxing. If someone is only a good boxer, a superior wrestler will defeat him. Or if someone is only a good wrestler, he may get knocked down before he even gets a chance to wrestle. If he's a great boxer but doesn't pay attention to his opponent's feet, he can get knocked out with a kick. And while the fighters are trying to pay attention to all that, they must be skilled in a whole spectrum of joint locks and chokes, or they could be forced to submit to a superior jujitsu artist no matter how good a boxer or kicker they might be. It's so complex that you never know what's going to happen next. The fight can change in an instant, with the fighter who looked like the sure winner suddenly becoming the loser. It's thrilling to watch and definitely not a sport for the timid. I love ultimate fighting. But . . .

Ultimate fighting is not ultimate.

"Our struggle is not against flesh and blood, but against the rulers, against the authorities, against the powers of this dark world and against the spiritual forces of evil in the heavenly realms" (Ephesians 6:12).

Now that's ultimate fighting. I believe God is challenging us to do something about the spiritual darkness that rules much of our world. And it's clear that the forces arrayed against us are demonic in nature, with a "mixed martial arts" strategy against us. In other words, though we may not understand all the specifics of the spirit world, we know that the powers aligned against us are diverse, attacking in different ways in different situations and with different strategies. If we want to counter this, it's imperative that we become skilled in "mixed spiritual arts" ourselves.

Of course, all of this is assuming that God is real and that what he says in the Bible is true. If you're skeptical about all this talk about demons and spiritual warfare, would you at least consider this? Would you want to worship God if he were to blame for the evil you see in the world? If God is real, doesn't the existence of agents of evil who oppose his work make good sense? And with examples of unfettered evil in our world such as terrorism, genocide, and the Holocaust, is it really such a stretch to believe that there might be something spiritual—and evil—behind it all? Just give it some thought.

For those of us who do believe in the reality of demons, it's clear that God has called his followers to battle. Much has already been written about spiritual warfare: some of it good, some of it pretty bizarre. But most of it overlooks any responsibility on the part of those who follow Christ to *act*. It mostly revolves around praying.

Now, it's abundantly clear that prayer is the first and most important line of defense in spiritual warfare as well as our best offensive weapon.

But not just any kind of prayer.

In one of the most stunning passages in the Bible, God basically told his people to stop praying. Don't bother. He's not listening. "When you spread out your hands in prayer, I will hide my eyes from you; even if you offer many prayers, I will not listen" (Isaiah 1:15). Now why would God say something like that? Doesn't he always want us to pray?

Not if it means that all we do as Christians is sit on our butts.

Maybe what disturbed God so much in the first chapter of Isaiah was that his people were *saying* the right things in their prayers but not *doing* the right things in their lives. He told them, "Stop doing wrong, learn to do right! Seek justice, encourage the oppressed. Defend the cause of the fatherless, plead the case of the widow" (Isaiah 1:16–17). And the next verse is the perfect example of how we tend to read Scripture through the lenses of what we want it to say, not for what it actually says. "'Come now, let us reason together,' says the LORD. 'Though your sins are like scarlet, they shall be as white as snow; though they are red as crimson, they shall be like wool'" (Isaiah 1:18).

Can you hum the old song? Some of you who have been in the church a long time know what I'm talking about, and the tune is running through your mind right now. It's a precious song to me, one I sang many times in the early days of my Christian life. But while we evangelicals have usually applied it to the lost coming to Christ, the passage is clearly directed to God's people. And it's not a call to repent of our lust or our lack of a "quiet time." It's a call to mend our broken relationship with God that renders us selfish and unwilling to care for the needs around us.

It's a call to repent because we've made no difference in combating the evil of the world. And it's not talking about the evil we normally think of or the way we normally think of fighting it. This is not a call to stop the homosexual agenda or to defeat the abortionists. It isn't about fighting political battles to get our candidate elected. Instead, it's about God's people waging war on the evil that destroys people—and the chance to heal the wounds inflicted by that evil.

If spiritual warfare were only about praying, it would be strange that Jesus was always touching real people, even the people no one else seemed to want to touch: lepers, thieves, cheats, prostitutes, and all the socially unacceptable crowd. Since Jesus prayed—and then went and changed the results of evil in the real world—maybe we should give that a try too.

I'm not claiming to give any kind of comprehensive teaching on spiritual warfare here, but I am challenging followers of Christ to consider an element of spiritual warfare that we've almost completely ignored—the actual, real-world defeat of the work of the Enemy around us through loving its victims and acting like Jesus.

Let's pray! Yes! Nothing is more important in my life or church than that. But then let's leave the prayer room. Let's leave the church building and go fight for real. *Amen* is the end of our prayers; it's not the end of our battle.

Amen is our invitation to war.

Amen means that now it's time to go to work.

That will put a scare into the forces of spiritual darkness that they haven't felt in a while. I'm afraid that the church has largely wimped out. We have thought that *boldness* meant preaching louder, sweating more, and saying just the right words to get the crowd shouting and applauding. But it doesn't take much courage to do that in front of a group of people just waiting for the cue to clap. I know. I've preached those sermons, learned those cues, and enjoyed that applause. If we truly want to be bold, let's go out into the real world, where the demons live. Let's spend a little time where drugs, crime, poverty, abuse, and fatherlessness reign. Let's see if we are courageous enough to quietly love the unlovely in the face of pure evil rather than shouting loudly to the applause of the choir.

Let's pray! But let's be "mixed spiritual artists" too. The Enemy has a pretty good idea of our strategy now. We don't seem to vary it much these days—at least not the vast majority of churches that are failing to reach their communities. We just try harder to do more of the same preaching, the same kind of evangelism, the same political efforts—with the same results. It's time to add to our arsenal.

Keep praying, but start serving. Keep preaching, but start touching. Keep evangelizing, but start transforming.

That kind of spiritual warfare just might knock demonic rulers off their thrones and bring real change from a real God for this messed-up world. A character in a great novel I read recently, *Sins of the Assassin,* says, "When a religion loses sight of what true evil is, it's no longer a religion, it's a bowling league."[5] Sound a little like the church today? Or maybe a lot? Then let's follow Jesus into the bloody, depraved world outside the church walls and stare evil in the eye—and then do something about it.

See the True Face of Evil

If we are to live as though God is real and work with Jesus to advance his kingdom by defeating the evil around us, then this fight must get personal. It's important that we really see the face of evil.

We think we've done a pretty good job of that.

But I believe we're looking into the wrong face.

Can you picture in your mind right now the face of someone who personifies the evil the church has opposed? Maybe it's Hugh Hefner or some politician or Supreme Court justice. I'm convinced that those faces will never motivate the church to defeat evil. For decades we have rallied around our causes and fought to defeat our opponents.

How's that working for us?

If we don't like the results of the culture war, then what should we change? Is it possible that we are missing one of the simplest, clearest teachings of the Bible that could be the one motivation that will allow us to really change anything?

"God so loved the world that he gave his one and only Son" (John 3:16).

And he did that for evil people. What have you given to love an evil person?

Could it be that rather than looking for people who are *perpetuating* evil, we should try looking into the faces of those who are being *destroyed by* evil—and love them? Could it be that love, not righteous anger, is the only truly biblical motivation that will make a difference in a fallen world?

Evil has a face. But not in the way we thought. We should not be looking for an evil person to stop but for a person destroyed by evil to love. That's the face we should be looking for.

A few weeks ago I was sitting at the desk in my office. I'm not terribly technologically savvy, but I had learned how to pull up a webcam on my computer. I love the Caribbean, and I discovered that I can look at a live scene from a Caribbean beach anytime I want to. Nothing calms my spirit on a busy day like a quick look at the warm sand and sparkling waters of a tropical island—just as if I were there.

Well, after I found this first webcam, I figured there must be others on different islands. So I searched for island webcams. (I won't tell you which island because I don't want you to do what I did!) I went to a site advertised as an island webcam and found myself looking into the eyes of a beautiful young woman. I quickly realized that this was streaming live. From across the world, she was staring right at me, right through my computer screen. She was fully clothed, but as I read what was written below her picture, I realized that with just the swipe of a credit card, she wouldn't be for long.

I am a fully heterosexual man, regularly tempted by sexual sin and fully capable—apart from God's strength—of using her like other men do. But that's not what happened as I looked into the eyes of this woman—barely a woman at all, likely a teenager. I looked into the eyes of evil. Not an evil woman but the evil destroying a woman. I couldn't break away from those eyes. They were almost dead: sad, lonely, abused, wrecked. I knew that those who were using her wanted me to want her. And I did. But not her body. I wanted her heart. I wanted to reach through that screen and somehow touch her. Not like other men had likely touched her—but as Jesus would. I also wanted to touch the demons that were driving this whole thing. I wanted to touch them with the fist of God. I wanted to drive them out of this life they were ruining.

Those eyes . . . I wanted to see the freedom, love, and joy that I see in the eyes of my own daughters, not so different from her in age. She was somebody's daughter too. Maybe her dad didn't care, but I knew a Father who did. And his love drew me to her.

She is the face of evil.

Do you have a face like that in your life? One that breaks you and compels you to care, to love, to do something? That's the face of evil you must see if you want to follow Jesus; the face that reminds you of what evil does to people Jesus loves; the face that reminds you that there's something you can do.

I could not help that poor girl I saw on my computer screen. But I can see faces that look much like hers right outside my door. I intend to do something about that—and to lead a church to do it with me. To do what we would do in an evil world, if God were real.

Love Your Community Again

We get excited when we read something in the Bible like the story of the Philippian jailer who was saved. And we should. God saved a Philippian. But why don't we get even more excited that God saved Philippi?! The most thrilling story of all history is how God used an unlikely band of Jesus followers to transform whole cities, until even Rome itself was changed. Without this miracle, you and I never would have heard of Jesus. It is crucial that we learn to love our cities again, to believe that God has called us to be a transformational force in our communities.

I preached on the Good Samaritan recently. I reminded our people that the Samaritan did a wonderful thing. But when he moved on, the road still wasn't safe for future travelers.

Who will make the road safe for travelers through your city?

This, I believe, is the great opportunity the church has been missing. We talk about changing our cities. What we usually mean is getting more people to come to our churches. That's not a bad thing.

But does that really change our communities?

Ask yourself. Has it? Has it done in your town what happened in Antioch? Or Philippi? Or Rome? If not, why not?

These are questions we're asking ourselves in the church I pastor. And we've determined that God is calling us to care about our community in a way we haven't before. We know that we're just beginning the journey to love our community as we should, but we believe in that mission. We're committed to it.

And though it seems impossible for an entire community to be visibly and positively transformed for good, we believe it will happen!

We believe it's what Jesus would do and did do. And we believe that he is real. What he does works. So here is the local vision of our church: we will give ourselves away for the transformation of our community.

The mess we are in began in a garden (Eden) but will end in a city. Cities are mentioned more than 1,200 times in the Scriptures! Cities are key in the heart of God and in the story of God in the Bible. Jesus wept over a city, and then he died there for its people. We want to see what could happen if we *live* for the people of ours.

We don't intend to back off of our passion for evangelism. In fact, we believe we'll be more effective than we have been in the past. People tend to listen to the good news when they see it in action first. But we believe that God has called us to actively love our city and to accept responsibility for every realm of our community, not just the areas we have viewed as "spiritual." The church should impact economic development, education, health care, law enforcement, and every other part of life. If we believe Jesus is Lord of all, why would we divorce him from these areas?

We don't seek to take over. We seek to serve—to give ourselves away. And we'll do it until we see the community transformed. We believe the community will be transformed when the King and his kingdom influence every domain of the city for good.

If we are truly after kingdom influence, then we will not be able to accomplish our vision as individuals. We were never intended to. Jesus clearly intended his people to act together as one body. It's the great tragedy of our day that so few local churches are actually developing a united strategy to transform their cities. It's unconscionable the power we are wasting!

We want to stop the waste. At our church, we are intense and intentional about loving and transforming our community by the power of God through the church united. We are rapidly working to bring pastors together to pray and break down racial barriers. We're actively and honestly assessing our divisions and the challenges of our community and asking God to show us his strategy that we can implement together.

The church does not have to reinvent the wheel. In every community wonderful, transformational organizations already are in place. But many are under constant financial pressure and seldom have enough volunteers. Churches have the opportunity to be both inspiration and motivation for transformation, as well as the network that produces synergy and focus among the different organizations and domains of the community. Eric Swanson writes, "The church then takes a *catalytic responsibility* for connecting and harnessing the energy, resources and horse-power of the other domains to tackle the problems of neighbor-hoods, schools (elementary schools are often used to define a neighborhood) and families—the smallest individual unit in a neighborhood. . . . The church can partner with any other domain and all domains based on their common love of the city . . . not theology."[6]

Jesus' words in Matthew 25 will be our guide for what we do to transform the community and how we will direct our activities and measure success. After all, this is what Jesus said would matter in heaven! "I was hungry and you gave me something to eat, I was thirsty and you gave me something to drink, I was a stranger and you invited me in, I needed clothes and you clothed me, I was sick and you looked after me. I was in prison and you came to visit me" (Matthew 25:35–36).

We know that these are not things that save us or earn God's love. We don't have to earn it. We have it! But loving people in the ways Jesus described is supposed to be everyday life for Christ followers.

Have you ever been at a conference and heard someone ask another pastor how his church was doing? The answer usually re-volves around baptisms, budgets, and buildings. Can you imag-ine hearing a pastor talk about the number of impoverished people the church helped lift from poverty, the number of racial and other barriers torn down, the number of sick people cared for, and the number of prisoners ministered to? The amazing thing is that if you ever did hear this, you probably also would hear whispers that the pastor must be a liberal. Why? If we be-lieve God is real, if we believe Jesus is Lord, if we believe the Bible is true, then here's a radical concept to consider:

Why don't we just do what he says?!

Hard to see what's liberal about that. To be clear, our church is not neglecting the gospel as we do this; we're *living* the gospel. We don't neglect the good news, we *become* good news. We don't stop inviting people to come and see, but we begin to go and show. And when we get there, we touch and tell—meet the pressing needs that others won't or can't meet and then always make sure we explain why we do it. We do it because we are followers of the God who loves our city, and we are joining him on his mission of love.

How will we do this? That's the big question. We believe that churches that want to be the body of Christ, to transform their communities together, will also have to learn together. Solving the tremendous problems we face is no easy task, and there are no easy answers. But if God is real, we must believe that he will show us a way.

Our church intends to start with neighborhoods. We'll partner with the elementary school and seek to change a generation of children. At the same time, we're developing a systematic way to help families out of poverty. Churches like Brooklyn Tabernacle and First Baptist Church of Leesburg, Florida, and many others are changing their cities in just this way.

We'll raise up community missionaries from within local neighborhoods and, if necessary, bring missionaries in. We'll mentor the children. But it's not enough to mentor them for an hour and then send them back to hell for the rest of their day. We'll use community missionaries in partnership with multitudes of volunteers to follow up daily with those we mentor. We'll love and offer freedom, hope, and a fresh start to those caught up in gangs and drug use. We'll work with law enforcement to drive out the drug dealers and the gangs. We'll make it impossible for perpetrators of evil to continue destroying lives in the neighborhood where we serve. We'll rebuild houses, plant gardens, and restore dignity. Even in the last month our church has met with an Assembly of God church less than a mile away from us. We prayed together like we believed in God. Then a few weeks later more than six hundred of us went into our neighborhoods together to mow the lawns of single moms, mentor children, paint schools, build relationships, find needs and meet them.

It won't be easy. We'll have setbacks and failures. But we won't back down. Living transformed and transforming lives is our birthright in the family of God. We'll commit to learning together, to educating ourselves about the needs of others whom we may barely have noticed before. And we'll pray—a lot! And God will work . . . because he is real.

Robert Linthicum describes well what we're striving to accomplish: "God's primary intention for the city is to bring God's kingdom into that city—to permeate its political, economic, and religious structures, to transform the lives of its inhabitants, to exorcise evil and unrepentant principalities and powers, and to place over that city, not a brooding angel but a Christ who would gather the city to himself. It is God's intention to transform every city into the city of God by making of that city the embodiment of God's rule."[7]

Find Yourself in a Messed-up World

It's easy to get lost in the pain of this world. I've watched people wander through the darkness of it all and lose their way. But that doesn't have to happen—not if we walk through it with the God who is real. Not only does the mess of this world make sense if the Bible is true, but it's possible to find ourselves—to know who we really are and what our lives are meant to be—because of the pain we walk through in this world.

Larry Jones is cofounder and president of Feed the Children. We were talking recently, and he told me a terrible story that could make anyone wonder if God is real. Women in Kenya sometimes leave their babies to die at a certain garbage dump when they can't feed or care for them. Larry's ministry finds these babies and saves their lives. Several years ago they were almost too late for one little boy: dogs got to him first. They mauled his face.

Who would adopt an African child with half a face? Larry Jones and his wife would. They are now halfway through twelve years of surgeries to restore their son's face. Recently he had surgery so he'll be able to smile for the first time.

Why would a God of love let such tragedies happen? I wish I had the answer. I just don't. The fallen nature of this world is real, and it has given rise to horrible suffering. But how can I not believe in God when I see the response of people like Larry and Frances Jones? What else but a God of love could explain their love for a child whom no one else cared for?

I asked Larry how he does it. How does he look into the face of this precious child every day and deal with that pain? Larry looked surprised. He said, "John, my son has more joy than anyone I know. And when I look into his face, I see who Larry Jones really is."

I'm still amazed by the power of that insight. Yes, there are awful things in this world. But perhaps one of the reasons God allows such pain is that when we look squarely into the face of it, with the determination to be used by God to heal it, *we* are changed. We see in the face of the victims of evil a mirror that shows who we really are.

Fallen, sinful, mauled and distorted . . .

. . . loved, healed, transformed, and commissioned.

This is life that makes sense when the world doesn't. This is life worth living with the real God.

7

If God Were Real ... You Would
Be Really, Really Rich

It is not what we take up
but what we give up that makes us rich.
Henry Ward Beecher

I F GOD IS real and what he says is true, we are rich beyond our
wildest imagination. Now, that's good news since as I am writing
this, our economy is coming apart!

We don't have to have lots of money, possessions, or financial
security to be rich. After all, if you have your health, you have everything, right? If you're happy, live a long life, get to see the
impact you've had on the lives of your children and grandchildren—doesn't that make you rich? But what if you don't have any
of those—none of the things that the world thinks makes one
rich? The fact that so many Christ followers like that still manage
to live full, really rich lives has to be dramatic evidence that God
is real.

Let me introduce you to one such woman. I'm grateful to
Richard Gates for allowing me to share this. Richard was the
chairman of the search committee that brought me to the wonderful First Baptist Church of West Monroe, Louisiana. Richard

is married to Paula, a wonderful woman and great Christ follower. Richard's first wife, Kathy, died September 8, 1994. I never
met her. But she was an amazing woman who really believed in
God and lived like the rich woman she was . . . and everyone
around her knew it. I know these things because I am holding
her letter in my hand: the letter she wrote to be read at her funeral. As I share excerpts of it with you, ask yourself, "Is such a
rich life in the face of sickness, sorrow, and loss really possible
apart from a real God?" And if, as I believe you will, you determine that the answer to that question is no, then use these moments to determine to follow this real God with all that you are,
for the rest of your life and forever.

Many of you will say, "Poor Kathy." She had so much to
deal with in her life. Well, I'm not poor Kathy. I've had
a wonderful life. I had really good parents. When I was
in college, Daddy was diagnosed with lung cancer. It was
a terrible time, and he was sick for two years. He died
when I was twenty-two. Several years later Mother was
diagnosed with ovarian cancer. I remember repeating the
verse, "In all things God works for the good of those who
love him, who have been called according to his purpose"
(Romans 8:28). I really didn't see how that was true. I
couldn't believe God was expecting me to go through this
terrible illness with another parent, and I surely couldn't
see anything good about it. I really thought God had
messed up with this one. Well, Mother was sick for about
two years. She died when I was thirty-three, and I've really
missed my parents.

So have I gotten to be "poor Kathy" yet? Not really.

Things in our lives can be terrible by themselves. But when we are called by God according to his purpose, they can be worked out for good.

When I turned forty, I didn't realize I would literally fall apart. But I did. That's when I was diagnosed with breast cancer and had surgery and chemo. I had one good year and then the reoccurrence. I was devastated. Now, right here, I may have been "poor Kathy." I thought, *Lord, what do you want from me? How much? How can this work for good?* I didn't see any way in the world that two teenage girls losing their mother could be turned into good. I am not afraid. I actually look forward to seeing Mother and Daddy and being with the Lord. I think it will be great. I know that God's grace has given me this feeling.

I can't be "poor Kathy." The Lord has given me too many blessings. And I can only imagine the wonderful things in store for me in heaven. I don't know why the Lord chose to give me total healing (which is death) instead of physical healing. I really think it is his reward for me. But I do know that he has changed the desires of my heart. I desire to do his will. If he wants me in heaven, I desire to be there. I have not just accepted the inevitable. I am actually desiring it. God always keeps his Word.

Many of you have told me how strong I have been. I'm really not. My strength comes from God through Jesus Christ and the Holy Spirit.

You've also said I've been a real inspiration. What have I inspired you to do? I hope you are inspired to get your life together with God's will. His peace and strength and comfort come only through your relationship with Jesus Christ. I don't care what Oprah says. There is only one avenue to God—through Jesus Christ. I want you to remember that I'm not afraid. I have loved my life. I've had a great life. I love my family, and I love all of you. Thanks so much for loving me too. I hope to see you all again.

Kathy Nelson Gates
January 13, 1950–September 8, 1994

I don't need to say much more, do I? That's what it is to be rich. Really, really rich. That's what it is to believe God is real. No matter what. That's what a follower of Jesus looks like. Some of you may feel you've never really seen one—until you read these words. Well, now you have. And I hope that a part of the response to Kathy's faith in the truth of Romans 8:28 is found in what you do in response to her life.

As for me, it is my desire and intention to live richly and to join the growing movement of those who are passionate to spread the riches around—so that no one misses out on this rich life with the God who is real.

I think 2 Corinthians 8:9 is one of the most beautiful verses in the Bible: "You know the grace of our Lord Jesus Christ, that though he was rich, yet for your sakes he became poor, so that you through his poverty might become rich." And the riches we have aren't affected by economic conditions. "Praise be to the God and Father of our Lord Jesus Christ! In his great mercy he has given us new birth into a living hope through the resurrection of Jesus Christ from the dead, and into an inheritance that can never perish, spoil or fade—kept in heaven for you" (1 Peter

1:3–4). In this life our riches make life new and full of hope. But we are also investing in an inheritance. And the return on the investment is guaranteed to beat every benchmark—forever!

On the other hand, if all this is real and we live like it's not, that is a loss of unimaginable proportions. It would be like burying our money and living in squalor, like paupers. Yet that seems to be the case for much of the church in this country today. One of the most shocking and ironic findings presented in the book *unChristian* is that while young outsiders largely believe in the supernatural world and believe it can be accessed, the last place they would look for supernatural power is in the church: "Christianity is perceived as separated from real spiritual vitality and mystery. It seems like a religion of rules and standards. Surprisingly, the Christian faith today is perceived as disconnected from the supernatural world—a dimension that the vast majority of outsiders believe can be accessed and influenced. Despite outsiders' exposure *to* church, few say they have experienced God *through* church."[1]

What a tragedy! It's one more reason I think that Christianity as we know it (at least as we know it in America) has to go. I wrote a book called *Authentic Power,* in which I shared many of my experiences in the persecuted church. There's no lack of power there! The wonderful friends I know in the persecuted church live incredibly rich lives full of joy and adventure—and at the same time full of risk and suffering. In fact, the way they live is, for me, one of the best evidences that God is indeed real. Besides God, there seems to be no rational explanation for the power and peace of these sufferers now and through two thousand years of the persecution of Christians.

Perhaps our problem is that the Christianity of America is

not a very good representation of what it was meant to be, but because we've been so blessed in this country with comfort and freedom, we assume that God is pleased with what we have done with his church.

But the church of the New Testament looks a whole lot more like the church in China or the Middle East than it does the church in America. So if we want to change that and join a movement that takes God seriously and lives the rich life that he intends for us to live, how would we go about that?

Take Eternity Seriously and Childishly

Obviously, the matter of whether there is life after death is serious business. Really, there's nothing more important for you to decide than what you believe about this, is there? If you believe you have an opportunity to live forever, that will have huge implications for how you live now. If the message of the Bible is true, then the nature of our life in the next world is determined by how we live our life in this one.

Christians don't believe we go to heaven because of the way we live here, but we do believe that the way we live here will dramatically affect how we live there. Jesus said, "The Son of Man is going to come in his Father's glory with his angels, and then he will reward each person according to what he has done" (Matthew 16:27).

We also believe that our time here, to prepare for the next life, may be short. Jesus said, "I am coming soon! My reward is with me, and I will give to everyone according to what he has done" (Revelation 22:12).

Can you see how deeply it would affect how you live now if

you really believed this—that your entire eternity will be impacted by this one brief shot at earthly life?

However, if you believe that there is no afterlife, that this is it for you, that there is absolutely no God, and that all this is nothing more than a great cosmic accident that will one day wind down and end with no meaning, just as it began with no meaning . . . that could have a profound effect on how you live here too.

The Bible is pretty blunt about this: "If there is no resurrection of the dead, then not even Christ has been raised. And if Christ has not been raised, our preaching is useless and so is your faith" (1 Corinthians 15:13–14). And the results of a worldview that sees only this world are disastrous: "If only for this life we have hope in Christ, we are to be pitied more than all men" (1 Corinthians 15:19). In other words, whether we are believers or atheists, if there is no heaven, nothing much matters.

In the intriguing novel *Blasphemy*, the character Hazelius says, "That's how it is with death. One day, bang. Everything's gone. Memories, hopes, dreams, houses, loves, property, money. Our family and friends shed a tear, hold a ceremony, and go on with their lives. We become a few fading photographs in an album. And then those who loved us die, and those who loved them die, and soon even the memory of us is gone. You've seen those old photo albums in antique shops, filled with people in nineteenth-century dress—men, women, children. Nobody knows who they are anymore. . . . Gone and forgotten. To what purpose?"[2]

That's one of the most powerful portrayals I've ever read of the despair of atheism. For those of you who are atheists or who are trying to find your way through all this, take a moment and really consider this:

If there is no God, if there is no afterlife, why does anything matter at all?

I mean really, think about it. I've read a lot of material by atheists who write eloquently and make excellent arguments, with many points that deserve a good answer. But I have yet to hear a single argument that made any sense at all to me about how and why, if God does not exist, anyone could or should live a life of selfless purpose.

My friend Lauren Sandler says, "It's madness that to live a life of meaning, one would be required to swear that a man was resurrected from the dead two thousand years ago, and that his dad created the earth a few thousand years before that. Obviously, plenty of us secularists build our own purpose-driven lives without God."[3] Lauren has done well with that. She has a wonderful husband and new baby. She is kind and gracious. Frankly, talking to her is far more uplifting and challenging than talking to many Christians. But I think even Lauren knows that this is a hard sell. She longs for atheists to have their own youth rallies and home groups and social-action movements. Why is that not happening? Because deep down in the heart of every atheist is the one truth that cannot be escaped: if they're right and there is no God, and thus no afterlife, then ultimately, nothing matters.

It can't be escaped. In the last words of Lauren's book, she challenges atheists and secularists: "This need not be our own end of days; we must rebuild our broken home with bricks of reason, under a roof of agape, and upon a foundation of enlightenment rock-hard enough to withstand the flood to come."[4]

But the truth is, apart from God, apart from an afterlife, nothing will withstand the flood to come.

The character in *Blasphemy* is exactly right. If God is not real, if all we have is this earthly life, everything you do, every thought you think, every great dream, every good deed, everyone in your family—all of it—will disappear forever, never to be remembered or to matter to anyone, anywhere.

So there's no valid call to even attempt to make a positive difference in the world. Take the issue of global warming for instance. Let's assume, for the sake of argument, that Al Gore is right about everything. In fact, let's assume that the whole scenario is worse than we think, and in one hundred years, half the land on earth will be underwater. Let's assume even worse. Let's imagine that all the mess we have made of the environment creates new diseases, and in two hundred years, all of human civilization is wiped out, gone.

So what.

"So what?!" you say. How can I even write those words? How can I flippantly act like it would not matter if the entire human race was . . . gone forever.

Because that is exactly what atheists are asking us all to believe is inevitable anyway! That everything in this world, good and bad, is doomed to disappear without any future or purpose or meaning.

Gone forever.

In fact, if atheists are right, global warming is the least of our concerns.

Universal warming is on the way!

The big bang is heating up still. The whole universe is expanding, and one day, billions of years from now, the expansion will speed up to the point that the galaxies and then the stars and planets and even the atoms that make up matter will be ripped apart.

Scientists call it the Big Rip.

Gone forever.

Everything. Nothing left. Not even matter. Which means nothing matters! Really, now, if this is our ultimate fate, and there's nothing we can do to cause there to be any lasting meaning at all in this world or in the entire universe, why does it matter if all this happens in two hundred years or twenty billion years?

We're just on a celestial merry-go-round. What difference does it make if we go around two hundred times or twenty billion times?

It just doesn't matter.

Ultimately, this is where an atheist finds himself or herself. It becomes difficult to make a case for anyone to do anything but just enjoy the fleeting time here like a puppy enjoys being petted. Our lives just don't matter anymore than that.

But if God is real, if what followers of Christ believe is true, then everything in life takes on real and lasting meaning. You want to live with concern for the environment? Who should want to do that more than those who believe that they have been made stewards of this planet, that what they do here matters forever, and that this world is a shadow of the new heaven and new earth to come?

Jesus offers a compelling vision and a real reason to live selflessly, seriously, and joyfully in this world. If there is any compelling evidence for God and for the truth of Jesus, why wouldn't you want that to be true? Especially in light of the alternative. A serious view of the next life produces serious stewardship of this one.

Or at least it should.

This is where it gets embarrassing to be a part of Christianity. If we would just live what we say we believe, the seekers looking for spiritual power, spiritual connection, authentic community, cultural relevance, and social responsibility and activism would find it all lived out to the max among the followers of Christ. But sadly, most of us just continue to live as though God were not real. We live much like atheists—our priorities and actions look like we believe this is the only life we'll ever have. Most Christians live and die without ever even attempting to lead another person into a relationship with Christ. It's as if we really don't believe that eternity is at stake for those we come into contact with.

When Christians get together to pray, it's rare that anyone will even mention the need for a friend to come to Christ. Our prayer lists are filled with sick people. It looks like we're more concerned with keeping people out of heaven than getting anyone in. The early church ran straight into risk. They knew they would likely suffer and die for their faith, but they knew about the life that lay ahead. And so they pursued Jesus and his mission at great risk. Most Christians today try to get as far away from risk as possible. It's as if we believe that this life is all there is.

Jesus had a lot to say about the importance of childlike faith. He said: "I tell you the truth, unless you change and become like little children, you will never enter the kingdom of heaven" (Matthew 18:3).

Jesus said that we must change. We must change our very adultlike tunnel vision on all the stuff of this world and begin to see with the simple faith, expectation, and joy of a child. Life in this world for a follower of Christ should be filled with passion and purpose for life here, but it should also be filled with excitement that a wonderful trip is just around the corner. We should live like a child who has been told—and believes without doubt—that a trip to Disney World is almost here!

I love to plan trips. It's something of a hobby of mine. I just took Donna on a getaway, and she mocked me (goodheartedly) for having a written schedule for each day, hour by hour. Pitiful, I know. But I wanted to get the most out of the experience! When my children were young, we planned a trip to Disney World. It was wonderful. When the big day came, no one was more thrilled than my young son, Trey, who was about four years old. He couldn't wait to see Mickey Mouse.

As we were about to board the plane to begin the journey, I said, "Come on, Trey. It's time to get on the plane." Suddenly he began to scream and cry, "I don't want to get on the plane! I don't want to get on the plane." We were surprised, because he hadn't shown any fear about flying for the first time. We finally figured out the problem when he said, "I don't want to get *on* the plane. I want to get *in* the plane and go to Disney World!" He didn't want to be on the outside, looking in!

When we arrived in Orlando and walked off the plane, he said loudly, "Where's Mickey Mouse?" He expected to see that mouse. He knew we were going to Disney World. He had no doubt about it, and he was ready for it.

We need that kind of childlike faith and joy. A great journey is coming. It makes sense out of all the stuff in life that doesn't seem to make sense. It is real. It is everything our hearts have longed for. It is the consummation of our belief that God is real. There's no reason to live outside of God's plan. It gives purpose to this life based on the coming journey to the next one.

It's time to get in!

Let's take eternity seriously and childishly at the same time and live like we are preparing for that journey.

Live in Extravagant Simplicity and Intense Peace

I love the story in the Bible of Mary, sister of Lazarus. She was a woman who really believed in Jesus. She couldn't get enough of him. In Luke 10, we read that she got on her sister's nerves a little when she couldn't pull herself away from Jesus to help prepare the meal. But Jesus loved her and affirmed her. Then Jesus raised her brother Lazarus from the dead. Now that was just too much—she was overwhelmed with the reality of who this man Jesus was and what he had done for her. So she kind of lost it. She acted in pure extravagance—what some thought was foolish waste. "Mary took about a pint of pure nard, an expensive perfume; she poured it on Jesus' feet and wiped his feet with her hair. And the house was filled with the fragrance of the perfume" (John 12:3).

If we believe that Jesus did what the Bible says he did for us, we will love him extravagantly too. Real Christ followers should be the most generous people in the world. We should be generous with our love, freely giving it not only to those we think deserve it but also to those who don't. We should be generous with our forgiveness, not easily taking offense, since we know that we have been forgiven much. We should be generous with our time, knowing that as we take time to care and love others, we are not wasting that time but investing it. And no one should be more generous with money than Christians. After all, since this world is not our final home and we are only here for a short time, there's no reason to hoard stuff here.

That doesn't mean that a follower of Christ can't have a lot of money. But that money is meant to be used to bless others. So one who really believes in God lives in relative simplicity. He may have a nice house, but he is not driven to get a bigger one. She may drive a decent car, but she is not driven to get a better one. Life becomes a beautiful mosaic of extravagance and simplicity. Simplicity keeps us from plunging into debt as many people do, always seeking the next toy that will finally make us happy. Extravagance allows us to truly enjoy our money by watching how people are blessed as we give it away. Simplicity allows us to focus on what really matters in life, and extravagance allows us to make that focus a passion. Simplicity guards us from wasting God's resources, and extravagance leads us to invest boldly in the business of God that bears eternal returns instead of pouring it all into the business of man, the returns of which are merely temporary.

One of the best evidences that we really believe in God is how we invest our money, especially if we have either a lot of it or almost none of it. People don't give away millions or the money they need to buy food unless they really believe in the God they're giving it to.

Understanding and truly believing how really, really rich we are opens our hearts to the intense peace of God that he desires all of his followers to know. Jesus said, "Peace I leave with you; my peace I give you" (John 14:27). But this peace is not just a calm or a Zenlike state. It is intense peace. "For he himself is our peace" (Ephesians 2:14).

Followers of Christ have the opportunity to live every day with the intense recognition that he, the creator of all, the sustainer of life, the one who conquered death, is with us for good. The reality of that and how that empowers and impassions life is intense! And the way it works in us can be quite mysterious, producing that joy and quiet determination that I have seen so many times in believers who are facing what seems to be unbearable pain and tragedy: "The peace of God, which transcends all understanding, will guard your hearts and your minds in Christ Jesus" (Philippians 4:7).

This is not theoretical. There are people who actually live this way. I know that for some of you who are not yet followers of Christ, you haven't seen much of this in Christians. That's our fault. But I assure you that people who live this way are out there. And they're not uncommon. It's just that sometimes they're drowned out by the more public lives of those who live as though God were not real. But these extravagantly simple, intensely peaceful people are there; often quiet and not interested in the spotlight, but there nonetheless. Powerfully and wonderfully there.

I wish I could introduce you to some of them, especially for those of you who have not had the chance to see many people who live like God is real. I wish I could have taken you with me just a few weeks ago to see Nell. I call Nell "my sweetheart." Don't worry, Donna knows all about her. Nell is a frail little woman in her eighties who is dying from cancer—and living richly. I met her the first day I preached as pastor at my church. She came to pray with me before the service, and her smile lit the room. I could tell even then that she was very sick, but there was so much of Jesus in her it was hard to notice the affects of the illness for long.

Nell loves everyone, and everyone loves Nell. She lives simply and gives extravagantly, though she doesn't have much material wealth. She prays for everyone else's problems and lives in complete peace about her own. If you ask how you can pray for her, she'll say, "Just pray that I always keep my joy."

During one of our church prayer meetings recently, we brought Nell to the front of the room, and everyone shared what she had meant to them, how she had blessed them and influenced them. She beamed the whole time. Later she told me, "That was so wonderful! I got to live to see my funeral!"

When I went to visit her in her home, she chided me for spending my time with her instead of with those who needed to encounter Jesus for the first time. But then she joyfully shared how much she was enjoying talking to Jesus these days. How close she felt to him as she got closer to death. She told me things, precious things, that Jesus was telling her as she sat at the table and talked with him just as she would have talked to you. But she was still very human, not someone whose spirituality was so lofty that you couldn't relate to her. She told me that in these last days of her life, she had taken up watching golf, something she had never played. She just enjoyed it, in the simple yet extravagant way she enjoyed all of life.

Nell died last week.

She sat in her chair and just went to see Jesus. Her funeral was a celebration of one who lived richly, one who taught us all how to live like God is real.

Just before she died, she had given ten dollars to a mission team from our church to help them take the message of the Jesus she loved to others. I wish you could have known her. I hope I've helped you know her just a little bit. She was nothing special in the eyes of the world. But she lived a life that you can live too— not a copy of hers but your own uniquely rich life, full of the real Jesus, full of his peace. And then one day, you can meet her.

For those of us who already claim to believe in him and this rich life he gives, it's way past time to give the world a lot more examples of that kind of life. To let them see whole communities living this life. To show them churches—real churches—made up of people who stop living like spiritual paupers, fighting over little bread crumbs and arguing like spoiled children, and start embracing the life of the real God.

When we do that, entire cities will be changed. It has already happened many times. The Bible contains many such accounts. Like the time a group of persecuted, suffering Christ followers fled to a city called Antioch and lived the Jesus life in the view of the whole city. They broke racial barriers by reaching out to Greeks. They settled there and let the people see how real Jesus was to them. They were known for their "good news." They shared it everywhere. Unbelievers, even though they lived lives of idolatry and immorality, didn't see the Christians as their opponents or their enemies. They received love, grace, encouragement, and truth from those Christ followers. And soon the city itself was changed, as "the Lord's hand was with them, and a great number of people believed and turned to the Lord" (Acts 11:21).

There is no reason this cannot happen again—and again and again—in your city and anywhere in the world where God's people live like God is real, like the ridiculously rich people they really are.

The bottom line is this: an authentic encounter with the infinite transforms all that is finite.

I pray that all of us who say we believe in God will know the transformation that comes when we act, together, like we believe it. And I pray that all of you who are still unsure about God will take the risk of faith that will lead you to this rich life.

8

If God Were Real . . .

He Would Believe in Atheists

(A Friendly Word to Open-Minded Skeptics)

"I . . . miss . . . him."
Atheist Charles Templeton, onetime minister and
roommate to Billy Graham, breaking into tears when asked
how he felt about Jesus.

YOU MAY NOT believe in God, but he certainly believes in you!
God loves you. It's as simple as that. Your lack of love for
him or even belief in him does not hinder that love; it motivates
him. Jesus said, "Suppose one of you has a hundred sheep and
loses one of them. Does he not leave the ninety-nine in the open
country and go after the lost sheep until he finds it? And when he
finds it, he joyfully puts it on his shoulders and goes home. Then
he calls his friends and neighbors together and says, 'Rejoice with
me; I have found my lost sheep.' I tell you that in the same way
there will be more rejoicing in heaven over one sinner who re-
pents than over ninety-nine righteous persons who do not need
to repent" (Luke 15:3–7).

Did you catch that? He seeks for the lost one "until he finds
it." You may have given up on God, but God will not give up on

you! He never stops believing in you, loving you, longing to welcome you home. In fact, you have a special place in his heart. Should you ever allow yourself to be found, there will be more rejoicing over you in heaven than over all the people gathered in my church this Sunday!

I believe God has a place of tenderness and longing in his heart that is uniquely reserved for atheists. He knows the pain an atheist must feel at the sense of cosmic loneliness that comes from believing there is no God, no ultimate purpose, no real meaning to life. And God knows that the atheist is wrong—that he is missing all that could be: that the void in his life could be filled in an instant. And God knows that there is a sense in which the atheist knows that God really is there. The Creator has built the knowledge of himself into even the atheist's heart. But it's buried deep, covered over by layers of doubt and hurt and all the multitudes of reasons believers have given him not to believe. The atheist can't easily access that knowledge of God anymore. And nothing breaks the heart of the Father more than his lost child.

Think about it this way: What if you had a son who didn't know you existed? You were his father. No, more than that, you were Daddy. This child was bone of your bone, flesh of your flesh, made in your image; but he didn't know you were there. Wouldn't you go to almost any extent, short of harming him, to show yourself to him, to help him see that you were real and that you loved him desperately? And if your child refused to believe you, denied that you were his father, and wanted nothing to do with you at all, would that stop you? Even if you had other children who knew you as Dad, who responded to your love, who loved you back, would it stop you from pursuing this one lost son?

Now, I know all this is contingent on the possibility that God is real. If he's not, none of what I've just written matters, of course. And nothing else does either. But that's such a disastrous conclusion when drawn to its ultimate end, wouldn't it be worthwhile for you to at least consider, in some new ways, the possibility that God is real? To open yourself to that possibility? Wouldn't it be an intriguing possibility, at least, to consider that if he is real, he is passionately seeking you; and if you'll only seek him, you'll find him . . . and in doing so, you will be found?

I can almost hear the anger welling up in some of you—the same anger I've heard from other atheist friends—"I don't need to be found! I'm not lost!" The concept of "lostness" disturbs a lot of people to whom Christians apply it. But it's not really such a bad word, is it? There's no shame in being lost. I've been lost many times while driving. Being the man that I am, I often didn't know or believe I was lost; but that didn't stop me from being lost. And it wasn't a bad reflection on my character when I finally stopped to ask for directions. It was good to be found. Being "lost" is not a character flaw that you have to feel insulted about. It's not like someone saying you're ugly or stupid or cruel. You just can't see the way to the place you really need to be. Being lost is easily correctable. You can be found.

I know this doesn't comfort some of you. You still don't like being referred to as "lost." Well, even though I think it's not such a bad term, and Jesus himself used it, I kind of agree with you. The problem is that I think we're all lost in one way or the other, and it feels somewhat arrogant for me to call you lost as if I were totally "unlost." In fact, let me point out to my Christian readers that often we're lost too. It's abundantly clear that God expects us to join him on his mission to find those who do not know that he is their Father. It was the last thing Jesus told us to do before he left this world (see Matthew 28:18–20). If we know that Jesus is out looking for the lost and wants us to come with him, but we're running as fast as we can away from that call and into all the stuff of our own lives that seems so important to us at the moment, are we not lost from him too? Are we not lost from his plan for us, from his purpose, from the life he created and found us for? When we run from our mission, are we not as lost as Jonah was in the belly of the fish? If we know the eternal importance of joining Jesus in his search, yet we continue to live as though it doesn't matter nearly as much as the next thing on our list, is there much difference between us and atheists?

We are lost—all of us, it seems—in one way or the other. Atheists are lost from the God who seeks and loves them. Most Christians are lost from the God who wants them to seek *with* him. In 2 Corinthians 3:2–3 it's clear that our lives can be a "letter from Christ," a living testimony of the power and reality of God. Our lives can be testimonies, "known and read by everybody." What message are atheists and unbelievers reading from the "letter" of your life? Is it a letter of condemnation or of God's love? And what do we call a letter that never reaches its intended recipients?

The church has become God's lost letter.

So here's an idea. While those of us who believe in God are examining our own lives and coming to grips with our own lostness, would those of you who don't believe in God be willing to examine the possibility of yours? Consider the possibility of God again, perhaps in a new way. Ask him, if he is real, to show himself to you. If you seek him in that way, I believe with all my heart that you'll find him. And you'll be found.

What Kind of God Do You Not Believe In?

That's the question that a brilliant young woman I know sometimes asks atheists. Her name is Perry Frost. She's a college student who doesn't look or act like your average Christian. She really loves to be a part of a more countercultural crowd, so she dresses differently from the average college student in our church. But she looks a lot like many of the students her age who don't go to anyone's church. Perry loves to love people. She has joined Jesus in the search for his children who don't yet know him—but not in some obnoxious, salesmanlike way. She just cares about people. Her relationships aren't based on whether her friends are ever "saved." But she loves to talk openly about her faith and encourage her friends to think deeply about their lack of faith.

"What kind of God do you not believe in?"

Think about that a minute. When I hear what many atheists think about God, I sometimes say, "Wow, I think I'm an atheist, too, then. I don't believe in that god either!" Is it possible that you're both right and wrong . . . that the god you've rejected really doesn't exist, but that there's another one who does? Could it be that many of us have so messed up the image of the true God that you can't see him clearly for the caricature of him that we've helped to create?

I mentioned the novel *Blasphemy* earlier. I'm sure that most Christians will hate this novel. I loved it! It's a devastating picture of the impression of God we've left with people. In one scene a scientist named Hazelius is confronted by a preacher named Russ Eddy. The preacher is angry at the scientist's research into the big bang theory. Here's an excerpt:

"God will punish you anew." . . .

"What do you mean by 'anew'?"

"I've been reading up on you. I know about your wife, who pornographically bared her body in *Playboy* magazine, who glorified herself, and lived deliciously, like the whore of Babylon. God punished you by taking her. Still, you do not repent." . . .

. . . "Tell me, Russ. You're the pastor of a mission near here?"

"That's right."

"To what denomination do you belong?"

"We're unaffiliated. Evangelical." . . . "We're born-again, fundamentalist Christians."

"What does that mean?"

"That we've accepted Jesus Christ into our hearts as our Lord and Savior, and we've been born again through water and the spirit, the only true way to salvation. We believe every word of the Scriptures is the divine, unerring word of God." . . .

"Do you believe that God will send most people on earth to hell?"

"Yes, I do."

"Do you know this for a fact?"

"Yes. The Scriptures repeatedly confirm it. *'He that believeth and is baptized shall be saved. He that believed not shall be damned.'*"

Hazelius turned to the group. "Ladies and gentleman: I give you an insect—no, a *bacterium*—who presumes to know the mind of God."

Eddy's face flushed. His brain boiled with the effort to come up with a reply. . . .

"You're so smart, you think the world started in some accidental explosion, a Big Bang, and all the atoms just happened to come together to create life, with no help from God. How smart is that? I'll tell you how smart it is: it's so smart, it'll send you straight to hell. You're a part of the War on Faith, you and your godless theories. You people want to abandon the Christian nation built up by our Founding Fathers and turn the country into a temple to feel-good secular humanism, where anything goes—homosexuality, abortion, drugs, premarital sex, pornography. But now you're reaping what you've sown. . . . God will visit his divine wrath on you again, Hazelius. *'Vengeance is mine; I will repay, sayeth the Lord.'"* . . . "I can't wait to get out of this godless place."

As the screen door shut behind him, Eddy heard the calm voice say, "The germ extends its flagellum to depart."

He turned, pressed his face against the wire mesh, and called, "*'Ye shall know the truth, and the truth shall make you free.'* John 8:32."

He spun around and walked stiffly to his truck, the left side of his face twitching from humiliation and boundless, fulminating anger.[1]

Well, doesn't that make you want to run to church? Wouldn't you love to have that guy over to the house for a few days? Wow! What a disaster that this is how so many people view Christians—and our God!

So let me be clear. I hope you will *not* believe in that God, that angry, strange, vindictive God who hates you. I don't believe in him. And I hope you won't believe in "Christians" who are like that either. I know some aren't too different from that representation, but they don't really believe in God either—not the God I know. They don't seem to know the God who loves and seeks; who bleeds and dies so we don't have to; who defends the poor, the orphan, the widow, and even the stranger who doesn't believe in him. When it comes to that other god, I'll be an atheist with you. And I'd much rather spend time with you than with the crazy Russ Eddys of this world. But what I would like most of all is to continue on the journey of knowing the real God—and to take that journey with you. I have met him, but I don't yet know him as I want to. Many things about him I don't understand, and frankly some things about him I'm not even sure I always like.

But he's real.

I know he is. He has shown himself to me in countless ways, and I believe he will to you too. Please don't miss the real God because some of the people who use his name are idiots. Given the utter meaningless of life if there is no God, wouldn't you want there to be a God who loves you and seeks you?

The purpose of this book is not to present all the evidence for the existence of God. You can find much smarter people and better books to do that. But I thought it might help for you to hear from one of those smart people: Mike Licona. I worked with Mike for a while at a mission agency. He's one of the most brilliant men I've ever met and also one of the kindest. That's a rare combination. He has debated some of the foremost skeptics in the world, such as Bart Ehrman. In my opinion, Licona simply devastates the arguments of his opponents, yet then he's ready to become their friend! That's what I love about Mike. His primary focus isn't winning a debate but helping people find rational reasons to be open to the God who is searching for them. I love that! We've asked the question in this book, how would we live *if* God were really real to us? Now consider Mike Licona's evidence that God *is* real.

God Is Real!
MIKE LICONA

My widowed mother-in-law comments often on a friendship she has with a single male friend of whom she is very fond. Her friend is out of town so often that no family member has ever seen him. Occasionally we tease her, suggesting that he doesn't exist outside of her mind. Of course, we don't actually question his existence. But we have not altered our lives in a manner that is dependent on his actual existence.

Many Christians live in a similar manner, affirming God's existence in word but failing to live as though powerful and intimate fellowship with our heavenly Father is attainable in this life. To an extent, this may result from our not being able to interact with God in typical ways—that is, through our five natural senses. In what follows, I would like to outline a number of reasons why having confidence that God truly exists outside of our imaginations is warranted. These reasons are philosophical, scientific, and historical in nature.

Philosophical Evidence. At some time most of us have asked the following question: if God created everything, then who created God? In tackling this question, let's look at our available options. Was God created by another? If this occurred, our question only gets pushed back: who created God's creator? This question would go on and on and on. Just as an initial act has to begin a long sequence of dominoes successively knocking others over, so there had to have been an "initial actor" who began the process that eventually produced everything we presently observe. Since there cannot be an infinite number of actors, the initial actor either was "beginningless" (i.e., eternal) or unintentionally just popped into existence out of nothing. The latter is absurd, since nothing is nothing and cannot produce anything. Therefore, the only option available is that the initial actor did not have a beginning and has always existed. So, although it can be difficult to conceive of a being who had no beginning, we see that it is actually a logical necessity. This initial actor is what we call God.

Scientific Evidence. Is there anything we can learn from science that can tell us about the initial actor who is eternal? In recent decades our scientific knowledge has advanced in remarkable ways. Many findings from molecular biology weigh in favor of the conclusion that life itself is the product of design. In other words, life exists on earth because someone wanted it to and made it happen!

Many may be surprised to learn that volumes of complex information have gone undiscovered for thousands of years, yet it is closer to us than the tip of our noses. Before the electron microscope was invented in the 1950s, scientists viewed the simplest living organism known to us (i.e., the cell) as being very basic. Under a microscope, scientists could detect fluid within the walls of a cell. In the middle was a tiny dot called the nucleus. If the simplest living organism is that simple, then what's so difficult about life evolving by natural causes? At least that is what was thought before scientists could examine the cell using more sophisticated equipment.

We now know that the nucleus itself contains numerous members that carry out varying responsibilities resembling those found in a major city: fire, police, hospital, transportation, and city hall. At the city hall we find DNA, which contains information that governs everything about our physical and emotional makeup. Our height, weight (well, we have at least some control over this), intelligence, speed, inclinations, and much more is programmed into our DNA. One of the scientists who discovered DNA is atheist Francis Crick. He claims that DNA is so complex that, even given an earth that is 4.5 billion years old, there was not nearly enough time for undirected and unintelligent processes to render the formation of a single DNA molecule. Of course, almost anything is possible. But the prudent prefer the probable.

This creates a tension for atheists: if life itself is not the product of chemical evolution, how did it get here? Crick attempts to solve the tension by proposing that aliens from a distant galaxy sent bacteria to Earth to get things started. The discerning person will immediately observe that this theory only pushes the problem of complex life back to an undetectable planet, of which there is no evidence. In fact, it compounds the problem, since it means that even less time was available for life to form and evolve to a high level of intelligence on that planet. The Christian can hardly be faulted for understanding the complex nature of life as being the intentional product of an intelligent designer who created our universe with life in mind.

Historical Evidence. Has the initial actor who is eternal and immensely intelligent revealed itself to us? The Bible claims that he has, in the person of Jesus of Nazareth, who died on our behalf and was raised from the dead. Despite the objections of skeptics, there is strong historical evidence of Jesus' resurrection, and this provides us with a good reason for believing this claim. Although skeptical scholars reject much of what the Bible claims, nearly all of them are in agreement that we can hold with certainty at least three facts pertaining to the fate of Jesus: his death by crucifixion; that his disciples had experiences that convinced them Jesus had risen from the dead shortly after his death and had appeared to them in both individual and group settings; and that Saul (who would become known as the apostle Paul), while in the midst of persecuting the church, had an experience in which he believed that the risen Jesus appeared to him and that this resulted in Saul's conversion to the faith he had tried to destroy.

Historians attempt to detect what happened in the past by forming hypotheses that attempt to explain all of the knowable facts. But some hypotheses are better than others at accomplishing this. For example, people who contend that the beliefs of the disciples can be explained by hallucinations have trouble accounting for the group appearances of Jesus, since hallucinations, like dreams, are private occurrences in the mind of an individual. I could not awaken my wife in the middle of the night and say, "Honey, I'm having a dream that I'm in Hawaii. Go back to sleep, join me in my dream, and we'll have a free vacation!" In a similar way, I could not describe a hallucination I was experiencing to my wife and have her join in on the same hallucination. Moreover, since Saul was persecuting Jesus' followers, he was not grieving Jesus' death. So it's doubtful that Paul would have been a good candidate for a hallucination.

On the other hand, the hypothesis that Jesus rose from the dead explains all three facts very nicely. Historically speaking, it is the best explanation of the provable facts pertaining to Jesus' fate. Other hypotheses are quite inferior to the hypothesis that Jesus rose from the dead. Accordingly, we can regard Jesus' resurrection as an event in history.

In summary, I have outlined a few reasons why the rationally minded person is justified in believing that God is real. While it is generally accepted today that the natural sciences cannot yield information that provides us absolute certainty about almost anything, we have observed in this little space that there is very good evidence from philosophy, science, and history that points strongly toward this conclusion. God is eternal, extremely intelligent, and has revealed himself to us in the person of Jesus Christ. We do not have to suspend logic in order to believe the gospel. The rational person can trust Jesus with the eternal fate of his or her soul. Those who do this may find additional confirmation in a sweet fellowship with God as they walk through life together.

I believe God is real, but not just any God. Mike reminds us of the overwhelming evidence that the God who is real came to us, gave himself for us, and conquered death! I met this God personally as a teen. I really wasn't looking for him, but he found me one night. He used a pretty girl who invited me to a church—First Baptist Church of Hendersonville, North Carolina. There I encountered God and was changed. I'm still changed. Oh, I'd been to church many times before. But perhaps like many of you, the churches I'd been to actually made it harder for me to see the real God. That night in North Carolina, though, I saw something different.

I saw a movement.

I saw a dynamic movement of students as well as a movement of adults who loved students and allowed them to worship like students. It was a movement led by people who were willing to do whatever it took to be part of that movement—a movement of people who really believed in God. The pastor of the church, Ian Walker, and Minister of Worship and Students, Aubrey Edwards, are still dear friends of mine thirty-three years later. They talked with me that day and prayed with me as I entered the relationship with God that has shaped every part of my life and continues to do so to this day.

Then I met Aubrey's cousin, a man named Dan Cathy, son of Chick-fil-A founder S. Truett Cathy. Years later, in the strange way that God puts things together, Dan became the president of Chick-fil-A, and I became his pastor. He's one of my closest friends, and as I think back over the amazing way that God has shaped and directed both of our lives, I'm again reminded that I would be a foolish man to attribute it all to an accident. I know that God is real. And so does Dan.

God Is Real
DAN CATHY

God has been real to me for as long as I can remember. God is real to me no matter where I am or what is happening around me or to me. I find it interesting that most of the objections to God's existence based on the problem of suffering come from people who have lived their lives rather comfortably. Most people who have experienced pain, suffering, or brokenness become stronger believers rather than stronger agnostics.

On Monday afternoon, April 29, 2002, I became a stronger believer. That was the day I went through what would seem to be an experience of pain and suffering. For me it was a life-enriching experience. I had the opportunity to experience God's presence in a profound way. I felt his presence right there with me.

My son, Ross, and I were burning piles of brush and debris from the property we were clearing for construction of our new home. We were using diesel fuel to light the piles on fire. When our supply of fuel ran out, I decided to try gasoline. Gasoline is, of course, much more explosive and volatile than diesel. But I thought it would be safe as long as the gas was soaked into the wood. This worked fine until the last pile—the one I lit just seconds after pouring on gallons of gasoline. I heard a loud *whvoooom*, saw the flames erupt, and felt an incredible wave of heat envelop me.

"Ross, am I on fire?"

"No, Dad, you just stay there, stay still!"

I knew something serious had occurred. I lay there in the grass unable to close my mouth because of the tightness around my lips. I looked over at my left hand; I could see rolled up, melted skin hanging beneath my wrist.

Emergency responders arrived and treated me at the scene. Then they ordered an airlift to Grady Memorial Hospital in Atlanta. I had extensive first- and deep second-degree burns on my face and arms, necessitating a variety of painful treatments and a ten-day stay in the burn unit. Thank God for morphine!

The moment I struck that match, my life came to a total standstill. I knew I should be experiencing panic, fear, or shock. Yet in the midst of that horrific event, I had total peace. I had God's peace. I knew that God was in control despite my unwise actions. I had confidence in the doctors and in the care I was receiving. I had nothing to worry about. Our heavenly Father is never caught by surprise—even when we make foolish mistakes.

God did not cause this event, nor did he have anything to do with my poor choice. My wife, Rhonda, said, "Don't blame this on God, Dan Cathy; that was just plain stupid!" Yet God used the consequences of my bad decision to teach me many things. In the Old Testament we read how God lit the burning bush and spoke through it to Moses in the wilderness of Egypt; I lit the burning brush, and God spoke through it to me in Woolsey, Georgia. In a sense, it inaugurated the second half of my life. My faith and trust in God only grew deeper as a result of that life-changing experience.

Not only did God become more real to me in my personal life, but I became more bold in expressing my faith at the office as well. As a businessperson and a Christian, I believe that God wants to influence my behavior and attitude at work. We need to see even our professional work as an act of worship, letting God fill all aspects of our lives.

Believers who have had a life-changing encounter with God will conduct themselves in the marketplace in ways that seem to defy traditional business logic. For example, many people cannot comprehend why Chick-fil-A is closed on Sundays. But we believe it honors God and the people who work in our restaurants, giving them a day off to spend with their families and to worship as they choose.

I have access to a treasure chest of principles in the Bible that guide me as I navigate through decision making. My wife and people who know me will tell you that I am still walking around in human skin. But reading and applying the Bible on a daily basis helps me recenter my life on God. Many biblical principles and teachings are so packed with marketplace relevance that they have found their way into my business approaches.

For instance, Jesus calls us to have genuine concern for the welfare of others and to serve one another with a cheerful spirit. He taught us to go the second mile in our relationships and interactions with customers and coworkers. So we at Chick-fil-A are changing the recipe for customers. We call it "Second Mile Service," based on Matthew 5:41. We're teaching team members to treat others with honor, dignity, and respect and to go above and beyond expectations.

Even our corporate mission statement at Chick-fil-A reflects our belief that if we acknowledge God, he'll direct our paths. Our purpose at Chick-fil-A is to to glorify God by being a faithful steward of all that is entrusted to us and to have a positive impact on all who come in contact with Chick-fil-A. We believe we should behave at work in a way that makes a positive impact on the lives of others. Our attitude at work should be uplifting, encouraging, and positive. We should practice genuine hospitality and glorify God by allowing his love to work in us and through us to an often tired, discouraged society.

God's existence is very real to me, and I aspire to let his principles influence every aspect of my life. I know God is real. He is just as real to me on Sunday morning at church as he is on Monday morning at the office. He makes himself known to me and reveals his truth to me through the Scriptures, giving direction, meaning, purpose, and fulfillment in life. God wants to do this in your life as well.

Now, I know that the fact that Mike and Dan and I have had life-changing experiences that proved to *us* that God is real doesn't prove to *you* that God is real. But when you look at the thousands of others who have had the same kind of life-changing experience, it starts to seem like pretty convincing evidence. That weight of evidence grows even more when you consider the number of staunch atheists—such as C. S. Lewis, one of the great intellects of the twentieth century—who have studied the evidence for God, and more specifically for the resurrection of Christ, and have become his followers.

Even such prominent scientists as Stephen Hawking admit that in light of the evidence, the existence of God makes more sense than his absence. But since the naturalism to which they subscribe precludes anything outside of nature, it's almost impossible for men and women who have given their lives to that philosophy to actually allow themselves to follow the evidence to its ultimate conclusion. If the evidence leads to a miracle, to God, they obstinately insist there must be some other explanation.

But for some, the evidence is so strong that they simply can't, with intellectual honesty, embrace atheism any longer. Antony Flew, for instance, the great British philosopher and lifelong fervent atheist, finally gave in to the facts before him and converted to deism in 2004 at the age of eighty-one.

Owen Gingerich, Harvard Professor Emeritus of Astronomy and History of Science, wrote the book *God's Universe* to show that the idea of a divinely created universe is not in conflict with science. In fact, as author David Aikman draws on Gingerich's research to explain, science actually suggests a creator who "finely tuned" the universe. For example, "at the time of the Big Bang, which cosmologists believe set in motion all subsequent developments in the universe, the balance between the outward energy of expansion and the gravitational forces trying to pull everything back together again had to be accurate to 10 to the power of 59. . . . It was exactly that, thus creating what Gingerich called a 'congenial' environment in the universe for self-conscious life."[2] For such precision to be achieved by random forces is not only highly unlikely; it seems scientifically untenable.

Francis Collins was an atheist before the evidence convinced him that God is real. Collins served as director of the National Human Genome Research Institute in Bethesda, Maryland, and wrote *The Language of God: A Scientist Presents Evidence for Belief.*

Those are some pretty good credentials!

If you're seeking truth in all this, consider: could it be that the existence of God and the death and resurrection of Jesus are overwhelmingly supported by the evidence but denied by militant atheists such as Richard Dawkins, Sam Harris, and Christopher Hitchens simply because they don't *want* to believe in God? When you read their books, it's surprising how hateful they sound toward someone they consider to be merely a myth! They spew venom at someone they say doesn't exist.

You might be wise to consider making a decision as important as whether you believe God exists based on something more than the opinions of people who might simply be angry with God and have, in a sense, taken out a contract on him. If the evidence points to God's reality, if the implications of his existence lead to a better life, and if he would actually do something to show you that he is seeking you, why would you not choose to risk faith? Simply follow the evidence (and yes, your heart) and choose to believe . . . and then to live like God is real.

At the beginning of this book, I issued the rather shocking challenge that if you can't find Christians who actually follow Christ, who actually live like God is real, then don't become one. I still stand by that challenge. In fact, I'll take it a step further. Why don't you ask God to—if he is real—bring you into contact with someone who can show you the reality of Jesus in his or her life? If God loves you as much as I say he does, if he has left the safe ninety-nine believers to come and find you, then surely he can lead you to someone who knows him—*really* knows him.

A woman named Trish and her daughter became a part of our church recently. Both of them encountered God in a radical way and were changed. Trish had been reading the Bible and seeking God for two years. She explains: "About two years ago, one of my questions to God was, 'These people you are describing to me in your Word . . . where are these people? I want and need to be with them. Do I need to sell my house . . . pack up and leave town? Just please show me where they are!'"

Wow. God heard her. He answered her. She found those people in a big church full of people mostly not even of her race. They are imperfect, but they are Jesus people—people who love God, love others, and really do believe in him.

Trish asked. God answered. You can ask. God will answer you too. He'll lead you to people who are authentic, really changed, followers of the real God. How do I know? How can I be so sure that God will do this for you? Because God *is* real! He promised that if you seek him, you will find him. And the real God keeps his promises.

My friend Lauren Sandler has been a part of many evangelical worship services in her research as a writer. But one night, at a youth conference in Colorado Springs, she experienced something she had not encountered before: what we evangelicals would call the work of the Holy Spirit. Lauren says:

By this time, I have heard the following sentence in hundreds of conversion conversations: "The worship band was playing, and suddenly I felt a brokenness inside and I couldn't stop crying." Well. The worship band is playing. Suddenly, I feel a brokenness inside. And I can't stop crying.

Despite my guardedness and my skepticism, was this to be the moment when I am born again? Has my long trip here been not my own journalistic investigation, but a path God has set to bring me to him? *Are you there, God? It's me Lauren.*[3]

I've read those words many times. Over and over. I love the vulnerability that Lauren showed in writing this, in shining the light on the inside of her heart and letting her readers see her struggle, her longing—yet, ultimately, not her conversion. She stepped back from that precipice, not ready to take the faith plunge that belief would have required. And though I don't base my friendships on whether someone is a Christian or ever becomes one, I can't help but want this for her. I want her to know that all of her intellect, her wonderful gift of writing, her graciousness, her family—all of her life—means something forever. And I want her to know the adventure of life with Jesus in the here and now. "Are you there, God? It's me Lauren."

He is, Lauren. He really is.

For any one of you who is reading this and is a seeker, haven't you felt that same pull on your own spirit? Maybe you even felt it as you read Lauren's words. I pray that you will take the risk of faith. Not blind faith, but reasoned, rational faith—yet faith nonetheless. Faith always requires a step into what looks, from where we stand, like darkness. I hope you'll take that step, that risk, and believe and step into what you will find is really that light.

And forgive us Christians—forgive me—for so often making it so hard for you to do it.

9

If God Were Real ... He'd Send Revival!

Revival is God bending down to the dying embers
of a fire just about to go out and breathing into it,
until it bursts again into flame.
Selwyn Hughes, *Revival: Times of Refreshing*

WE ARE ALMOST done with our journey together to see what life might be like, what might change, if we actually lived as though God is real. I devoted most of the previous chapter to our friends who are atheists or seekers. In this final chapter I want to talk to believers.

In spite of the mess we've made of Christianity, I'm actually an optimist when it comes to the Church. I don't see much hope for the system of Christianity, but I see great hope for the Church. My hope lies in the biblical and historical fact that God has never let his people go too long without sending a spiritual movement among them that brought them back to who they were meant to be. We often call these movements revivals. I've already said that we do not need a reformation or renewal within Christianity but a revolution or a rebellion. Or both. I like the new book *Do Hard Things* by eighteen-year-old twins Alex and Brett Harris, in which they call students to become "rebelution-aries."

The Church, with a capital *C,* is different from the religious system we've come to know as Christianity. Jesus died for the Church, not the church—not for a religion or institution. The gates of hell will not prevail against the Church. She is the bride of Christ. But she badly needs marital counseling! The Church must become again who she was meant to be—and fast.

I'm thankful for the great contribution George Barna has made to the kingdom of God. I respect him and, like countless others, have benefited from his research and insight. Yet I'm concerned about some of what he says in his book *Revolution.* Though I would agree with him at almost every point on the state of Christianity, his prescription seems to be to do away with the local church. Before we abandon it, I think we should try actually being the Church—the way it's supposed to be. I'm not sure most churches have even been part of the Church in recent decades.

Barna claims we "made up" the local church.[1] Yet the New Testament gives us many insights about how those first followers of Christ did church: how they worshiped, how they sang, when they met, how they implemented discipline, how they handled controversy, how they took care of the widows, how the church is to be led, and who should be the leaders.

I believe we need the local church. But we need Christians to rebel against what we have allowed our churches to become and against the system and human traditions of Christianity that often control and stunt them.

We need revival.

Historically, revival first changes Christians and churches and then changes the entire culture. Though I have significant concerns about Jim Wallis's new book, *The Great Awakening,* it's an important book, and he understands the significance of revival movements. Wallis writes: "There have been other periods in history when faith tangibly changed things. Often called 'Great Awakenings,' they are times when the 'revival' of faith alters societies. In fact, the historians say that spiritual activity isn't called revival until it changes something, not just in peoples' inner lives but in society."[2]

The power of these movements in the past is hard to overestimate. As I briefly discussed earlier, they have changed the course of the history of our nation more than once. And God promises that he will do that again—if we are ready to turn from the broken state we're in.

"Repent, then, and turn to God, so that your sins may be wiped out, that times of refreshing may come from the Lord" (Acts 3:19). If God is real, if he keeps his promises, then there's tremendous hope for the Church! Indeed, that hope is the hope of our whole nation—and the world.

If God is real, and if his people begin to believe it and live like it . . .

Revival is coming!

"In this City, we have beheld a sight which not even the most enthusiastic fanatic for church-observances could ever have hoped to look upon; we have seen in a business quarter of the City, in the busiest hours, assemblies of merchants, clerks and working-men, to the number of some 5,000, gathered day after day for a simple and solemn worship. Similar assemblies we find in other portions of the City; a theatre is turned into a chapel; churches of all sects are open and crowded by day and night."[3]

What great evangelical magazine do you think that quote came from?

Wrong.

It's from the March 20, 1858, edition of the *New York Times*! The secular world couldn't miss what was happening during that great revival.

Another observer wrote, "Revivals now cover our very land, sweeping all before them, as on the day of Pentecost, exciting the earnest and simultaneous cry from thousands, What shall we do to be saved? They have taken hold of the community at large to such an extent that now they are the engrossing theme of conversation in all circles of society. . . . There is a most astonishing interest in all the churches. . . . The large cities and towns generally from Maine to California are sharing in this great and glorious work. There is hardly a village or town to be found where a special divine power does not appear displayed. It really seems as if the Millennium was upon us in its glory."[4]

This is the kind of powerful impact that revival movements have had and can have again. And I believe that America is ripe for another Great Awakening. It's amazing how many people see this coming in the near future—people from polar-opposite perspectives: George Barna, Lauren Sandler, Jim Wallis, and many more; sociologists, atheists, liberals, and conservatives are all predicting a great spiritual movement that shifts and shapes culture.

Why this expectation? Well, there's little doubt that we're living in one of the most spiritually receptive periods in history. Everyone seems open to spiritual things. I often joke that the only people who aren't talking about Jesus today are Christians! We're afraid we might offend someone. But over coffee at Starbucks, everyone else talks about him and the latest book or movie or weird *Oprah* show about him.

I believe one of the reasons the New Atheists are so fired up is that it's clear they're losing the masses. They get a hearing, and people buy their books, but society at large is not buying into atheism. People aren't rejecting God or Jesus—but they are rejecting much of Christianity. This provides a great opportunity for revived churches to feed this spiritual hunger with something real.

Another reason I believe we're ripe for revival is the new breed of Christians I meet everywhere I go these days. I preach the way I've written in this book, and though I know this should be pretty controversial, I don't get much opposition when I speak. I think most of our churches are really starting to understand how much trouble we're in. And many are ready to do something about it.

The generation of young leaders in the Church today is not interested in much of what we've been doing in the past or how we've done it, but they're very interested in actually living as though God is real. I agree with Barna's assessment of this new generation of Christian leaders: that they have a "complete dedication to being thoroughly Christian by viewing every moment of life through a spiritual lens and making every decision in light of biblical principles. These are individuals who are determined to glorify God every day through every thought, word, and deed in their lives."[5]

Now that's encouraging! We have real hope—real reasons to believe that we could see revival in our day. I wrote a book called *The Passion Promise,* in which I looked carefully at the promise of God in Ephesians 3:20–21. It's my "life passage." When I was preparing to come to my new church to pastor, I was working on my first message—from this passage—when the mail came. One of the members of my new church, Bill Nelson, sent me a picture. When the new worship center had been built, he had chaired the building committee. Before they put carpet down on the platform, people were allowed to write scriptures on the concrete. His picture showed me what he had written. It was Ephesians 3:20–21: "To him who is able to do immeasurably more than all we ask or imagine . . ."

Bill had written those words directly under the place where I would stand to preach them!

Now, every Sunday, I stand on my life passage as I share the Word of God with our people. Sometimes I doubt whether I'll live to see a Great Awakening—to see the Church actually live out what we say we believe. But then I remember those words that I stand on—God's Word.

And I believe.

So what's God waiting for? If he wants to revive our churches, why doesn't he just do it? Well, revival is definitely a sovereign work of God that we don't always fully understand. But one thing seems always to be true about revival: God doesn't send it until at least a remnant of his people are ready to know what to do with it. God *always* uses people. He appears to have no Plan B. He waits until enough people within his churches will live as though he is real to facilitate the spread of the movement he wants to give us.

So allow me to conclude this book with some humble suggestions for the Church. You've read this book. You don't want "Christianity as usual" anymore. You want to see the power of God in your own life, but even more, you want to see it in a church that touches its community and beyond like the church of the New Testament did.

Here are some steps for you to consider.

Find a Movement of Jesus Followers and Pour Your Life into It

You may have to leave your church. I really hate to say that. I don't want to see people skipping around from place to place. That's not healthy and not what I mean. But life is too short to waste decades of it on churches that are really just clubs or family feuds. Don't be the grouchy church member who fights about everything. Just decide if your church actually is a church. If not, do a significant number of people actually want it to become one?

Ask yourself these kinds of questions about your church:

- Does the pastor want the church to live like God is real?
- Is he or she willing to risk the dangers of change?
- Is the church willing to make hard choices without wasting months or years arguing about every one of them?
- Is the church actually interested in loving and serving people rather than just meeting the members' needs?
- Are there signs that the church is determined to do what it takes to love, engage, and reach the unchurched?
- Are there leaders who will pray as though God is real and then do what God leads the church to do—even if it changes everything?
- Would you want to be at your church if you had never been in a church before?
- And if the answer to some of these questions is no, do you see hope for change in the near future?

If you honestly think the answer to most of these questions is no, then I believe you should begin looking for a group of authentic followers of Christ who are ready to be an authentic church. I know this is hard to hear, but we just don't have time to waste anymore. If your church would have to answer no to most of those questions and is not going to change without major warfare, it's going to die anyway. If you stay, you'll only join the funeral procession. So don't get mad. Don't waste your time trying to change it. Just quietly go. And you'll probably be surprised to find churches near you that—though not perfect—are actually determined to say yes to those questions.

The kingdom of God is doing just fine, and the Spirit of God is freely moving in many places. If you're in a church like that, I urge you to overlook the little stuff. Don't be a complainer. Pour your life into striving to achieve the big mission. Follow your leaders—and wherever God chooses to put you, become a leader yourself. Don't just go to your church on Sunday. Find the place where you can *be* the Church every day—and invest your life there.

Stop Praying for What You Want and Listen to God

Many dead, clublike churches pray a lot. Some of them even pray for revival. But here's the big problem you can't afford to miss: most Christians think revival means having the church become what they like again.

When Christians pray for revival, often they're really praying for a return to the good old days—which inevitably means a return to "my" day. We remember when we liked the music the most, the preaching touched us the best, or the sanctuary had that look that made us feel close to God. But none of those things has anything to do with revival.

Praying for God to do again what he did in the Great Awakenings or in any other period of revival has its own danger. Like all the best artists, God seems uninterested in repeating himself when he works. We see his amazing, almost ridiculous variety in the Bible: God spoke through a burning bush, a donkey, angels, and various weird prophets—including one who had just been spit out by a fish.

You just can't pin God down or put him in a box of your own expectations. He doesn't do things like he used to. He does whatever is best for each new situation. Revival today is not going to look like it did in the 1950s or the 1850s. When it comes, it will reflect the world as it is today—and how it will change tomorrow. God has done a good job of sending movements that directly impacted the issues of the future. The First Great Awakening was a crucial precursor to the American War for Independence; the Second Great Awakening brought understanding necessary for the abolitionist movement that led to the abolishment of slavery; the Third Great Awakening sustained the nation through the horrors of the Civil War; the Fourth Great Awakening, in 1904–1905, steeled people's hearts to endure the Great Depression and two World Wars. Funny how that works, with his being God and everything. He sends a revival that blesses the church today and raises up the kind of leaders the Church—and the world—will need tomorrow. He's the same God yesterday and forever, but he sure likes singing a new tune!

Here's the plain truth about revival. The essence of a genuine prayer for revival is this:

God, change everything about me that you need to change. Change everything about our church too. Do in me—and in your people—whatever it takes to bring you honor and glory. Help us to be willing to do whatever it takes to fulfill your Great Commission. Even if it means I never like another song I sing or sermon I hear in this church, may we do things that will bring this community to you. May I never get my way on a committee or like the kind of people who come here or the times of the services or anything else if, instead, we can reach people who aren't yet here. Bring this kind of revival to our church, Lord. In Jesus' name, amen.

That's prayer for revival. Most churches will never experience revival because they will never pray this prayer. And those churches will die. But yours doesn't have to!

Stop praying for what you *want* long enough to listen to God. Are you even praying for what *he* wants? Stop praying about what you want to pray about and see what God is telling you to do. And then do it.

Start *Really* Praying Again

When you've heard from God and broken out of your self-centered prayer rituals, now is the time to really begin to pray. Start a prayer meeting where you don't know exactly what will happen. Trust God to bring real needs to the forefront. Pray for the big needs of the community. Pray for people to come to know Christ. Call people up and pray for their ministries at work or in their neighborhoods. Share the answered prayers and the miracles

God does. Start groups that will pray the kind of revival prayer I just shared.

Ask God for a "lifetime prayer": something you will seek God for, along with others, until you see it with your eyes—or for the rest of your life. Protestant Reformer John Knox prayed, "Lord, give me Scotland, or I die!" Who is praying that for your community? You be that one! In our church, for years Billy Foster has "prayer walked" every street in our community. Now many others have come alongside him, and we're seeing the fruit of real prayer. If God is real, pray as though he is!

Guard Yourself against Popular Distractions

This is hard. Lots of things the church can do today will be popular and win applause from other Christians but won't keep us focused and ready to experience revival. Don't join every crusade against every sin in your city. I've been guilty of this at times. If we want to see our cities reflect the holiness of God, I think there's a better way than fighting everything and everyone we perceive to be in our way. If we persist in an almost militaristic approach to sin, two dangerous things happen.

First, we may begin to lose sight of our own sin. Jay Strack, one of America's leading experts on students, says that a new generation is not interested in our old position of "Love the sinner, hate the sin." They haven't seen any evidence that we love the sinner yet. So they want to see us "love the sinner and hate our own sin." I like that.

Second, we may make the unchurched whom we oppose think that, in order to become Christians, they have to become traitors to their cause. Unbelievers should feel drawn by love that opens wide its arms to welcome them, as Jesus drew Matthew and Zacchaeus and the woman at the well. Making people feel that God won't welcome them unless they join what they have long believed is the enemy camp is no way to draw the unchurched to God.

We may have made mistakes in aligning too closely with political parties. Be careful about this. We should have seen enough by now to know that neither the Republicans nor the Democrats have ushered in the kingdom of God. Jim Wallis wrote a fascinating book, *The Great Awakening,* to which I referred earlier. I love his premise that the coming revival will center on taking the love of God into the real lives, and meet the real needs, of people. Wallis is absolutely right that every revival changes society and that evangelicals have largely forgotten about the vast number of Bible passages that address issues such as poverty and injustice. But the book almost gets comical when Jim claims to be calling forth a new balance between conservatives and liberals—"conservative radicals," he calls them—and then makes it impossible to find anything conservative in the rest of the book. What I took away from the book was that, in order for revival to come, we have to reject the evils of George Bush, raise taxes, welcome illegal immigrants, and oppose the Iraq war.

Huh?

It's easy to be so tied to our own political convictions, conservative or liberal, that we're blind to the fact that other committed believers may disagree. Rather than getting entangled in politics, a better way is to pour your life and your church's efforts into actually doing something about the real issues around you instead of just complaining about the politicians.

Get Missional, Not Oppositional

I could hardly believe it: Wallis wrote a whole book about revival and barely mentioned evangelism! Regardless of that omission, the Great Commission still applies. No revival will come to a church that does not actively love and share the gospel with those who don't yet have a relationship with Christ. Rather than fighting and opposing everything we don't like in our society, let's go offer something better!

But Wallis does hit the nail on the head when he says: "The real difference today is not between evangelical churches and liberal churches, but between churches that are settled and those that are missional."[6] Yes! Liberal churches and settled, satisfied conservative church "clubs" are both moving toward the same end: death.

So get missional. Don't wait for someone to ask you. Join God in his mission to transform lives and communities, and take friends with you. At our church, we ask everyone to work to heal one wound. We want everyone to know that some ministry in their lives touches a real need in our community. We mentor children. We operate a thrift store for the needy and provide counseling services at low or no cost. We repair homes and clean neighborhoods to change the dynamics of depressed communities. We provide positive activities and teach life skills to teens who get little guidance at home. We take families through a coaching program to help them make decisions that will help them escape poverty. A few of us serve as chaplains for the police department, and we meet openly with the leaders of our city to work together to address the real problems and issues of our area. In all of these things, we always seek to be sure that we do it because of the love of Jesus in us.

We regularly feature these ministries so our people can see the opportunities available to them. Sometimes we have representatives of these groups set up booths after worship so people can sign up to help. We give of ourselves to help others, with no strings attached; but we never do it without telling the people why we help.

Here is our evangelism strategy. I think it's a good one for any church today to consider: *Come and See, Go and Show, Touch and Tell.*

Contrary to what some say, plenty of people will still come to Christ when you simply ask them to attend a worship service with you. That's *Come and See.* But it's not enough. We want to get outside our church walls and involve all of our people in ministry that shows the world the love of Jesus and a church that lives as though God is real. That's *Go and Show.* But that's still not enough. We must touch people's lives personally and tell them why we do it: because Jesus came to us in our own mess, and we love him, and he gives us love for others too—a love that they can know personally. That's *Touch and Tell.*

It's hard to break away from the oppositional mode. Some situations definitely require Christians and churches to take stands that may be controversial, but that shouldn't be our default position within our communities. Taking the hard line of opposition doesn't seem to be the biblical norm for the Church. Like the New Testament church (see Acts 2:47), a church today that lives as though God is real should have favor with the people of the community.

Recently I showed our church a video of Oprah's latest guru. Oprah denied that Jesus is the only way to heaven and spouted the usual New Age silliness that she has become known for. Then

I showed the church excerpts from her online classes, where she has become, in essence, a New Age evangelist. I asked, "How many people are mad about this?" Almost everyone raised his or her hand. Then I said, "Well, stop it. Why should we be surprised that the unchurched world is running after something spiritual when the churches have failed to give them the real Jesus and his love? If we don't like what Oprah is teaching, let's get out of here and go show the world something better." It was pretty quiet.

This is not easy stuff, but we're not after "easy." We're after revival. We're after a church that is worthy to be called the bride of Christ. We're after a church that lives as though God is real.

Stop fighting the world. Go love Jesus and people. Go get missional and do your part.

Be Creative Mavericks, Not Guardians of Tradition

In every great revival God has raised up leaders who were viewed by some as radicals. The greatest opposition to revival has always come from Christians. The unchurched world and, of course, many hungry Christians run toward revival when it comes. But almost invariably, traditionalist leaders of Christianity oppose change. John Wesley preached outdoors to the masses and was despised for it by many in the Church of England. Billy Graham refused to preach in cities that would not racially integrate his crusades. George Whitefield rode into Boston to preach to twenty-five thousand people and was met by pastors from the city. They said, "Mr. Whitefield, we are sorry that you have come." "So's the devil," he retorted, and rode on in!

Don't be stopped by resistance, and certainly don't *be* one of the resisters when God has something new for your church.

Are you satisfied with how things have been going? Are you a part of the transformation of your community? No? Then don't look to do the same old stuff, just doing it harder and hoping for better results. Ask God to birth within you his new dreams. If he is real, if he is the Creator and you are created in his image, don't you think he'll give you his creativity? Dream together with other missional believers, and follow the great Adventurer into his new day for you!

Center Your Focus on Children, Students, and Their Families

This doesn't mean you ignore senior adults or others. A church that does not care for the real needs of its seniors, and anyone else for that matter, is not a biblical church. But the truth is that most of our churches now cater to the internal church-centered needs of senior adults because most of our churches are full of old people. Now, there are really only two paths to take here: the senior adults can be spiritually mature adventurers for God who empower their pastor and leaders to go get their grandchildren's generation, even though it means they won't like all the music, etc.; or they can oppose all that, tell their grandchildren to go to hell, and play dominoes in the fellowship hall until they die and the church dies with them.

I'm blessed to pastor a church full of senior adult adventurers!

Whatever it takes, we have to reach this young generation, or we're committing ecclesiastical suicide. The generation born between 1984 and 1996, or the millennials, is the largest population group in the history of our country. And our churches are losing them. In my own denomination, we lose 70 percent of our active members between the ages of eighteen and twenty-two. They've been active in our churches, but then they leave high school and leave church too. Yet we seem to be better off than Christianity as a whole, which seems to lose about 80 percent. I guess Southern Baptists may be among the healthiest in the hospice. But that's not what we're after if we really believe in God.

Our church just broke a long-standing tradition and moved to a contemporary worship service for children and their parents. I can't tell you what changes your church may need to make, but if you look at your statistics and find no rapid growth among this age group, that has to become a top priority in your church. If you're not reaching a young generation and your church is graying, none of the rest of the stuff you're dealing with will matter in twenty years or so when the church is gone. Jesus called the little children to come to him. Join Jesus in that calling.

Develop a United Strategic Kingdom Vision for Your Community

This is among the hardest and most exciting steps you can take. In Jeremiah 29:7 God encouraged his people: "Seek the peace and prosperity of the city to which I have carried you into exile. Pray to the LORD for it, because if it prospers, you too will prosper." What an amazing verse! God doesn't say to hate the evil pagans or oppose them or fight them. He says to seek peace and prosperity for them and pray for them! He even identifies that as a key to our own prosperity. Does your church have any strategic vision from God for making a difference in the real issues your city faces?

Jesus prayed something else for his followers that we also seem to ignore: "May they [believers] be brought to complete unity to let the world know that you sent me and have loved them even as you have loved me" (John 17:23). The spirit of competition, envy, and selfishness among our churches is shameful. We might as well spit in Jesus' face and tell him to leave us alone. He has clearly spoken, and we have completely disobeyed. This may be one, if not the biggest, reason we have not seen revival in so long. God has never sent a Baptist Awakening or a Pentecostal Awakening or a Methodist Awakening. God brings great movements to the *body* of Christ, not to his toe or his spleen or his kidney. We need one another, and Jesus will not pour out his power on us until he can trust us to use it together.

We don't have to have uniformity. In our city, we're working hard at obtaining unity, but not uniformity. I will never agree about a lot of things with my buddy Mark at the Pentecostal church or Shane at the Assemblies of God church or Larry at the Methodist church. But we sure agree more than we disagree. And we are not the enemy! So we've decided to do whatever it takes to tear down divisions between us and between our churches. We're developing a united strategy to transform our city through prayer, evangelism, and the active love of Jesus. Together we're shattering racial barriers like never before in Louisiana. We're going after crime, poverty, addictions, and family disintegration. We intend to love one another desperately, defend one another intensely, and stand with one another strongly while we link arms with other leaders in our community until no one can miss the change. We have no doubt that this change will come: we're already beginning to see it. We're assured that we will see revival. Why? Because we have decided to believe God—and to live like we do. I hope you will join us in your city.

Join the Movement of the Real God

Christianity is broken. Irreparably so, I believe. But that's no hindrance to God. It has been broken before. But the real God has done an amazing job through the years of bringing beauty into brokenness. From the ashes of Christianity, this movement of the real God is rising. It's a little messy right now, as new movements tend to be, but the movement has a pretty good leader: the Holy Spirit, who is worthy of our trust and patience. If you join this movement of individuals and churches who have decided to live—no matter what the cost—as though God is real, expect to encounter speed bumps, barriers, and dangers. The pendulum will swing too far this way or that. Leaders will make mistakes. The movement may divert a little here or there. But stay the course. God is at work. Don't miss out!

In April 2008 the Western Oregon University women's softball team was playing Central Washington University. CWU had to win to make the playoffs. With two runners on base for Western Oregon, Sara Tucholsky came to the plate. She had never hit one over the fence in high school or college, but this time she uncorked the swing of her life, and the ball cleared the center-field fence. It was a game-winning home run. But as she rounded the bases, with all the celebration going on, she missed first base. As she went back to touch the base, she collapsed with a knee injury. She was in agony and couldn't get up. The first-base coach informed her that if her teammates helped her, she would be called out. The umpire said that if they replaced her with a pinch runner, Sara would only get credit for a single, not the game-winning three-run homer. She tried in agony to crawl to second base, but she could not.

Then something stunning happened. The CWU first base-
man Mallory Holtman and shortstop Liz Wallace—players from
the opposing team—picked Sara up and carried her. As they got
to each base, they lowered her good leg to touch it. When they finally reached home plate, ending their own team's chances of
winning their division and advancing to the playoffs, both teams
were in tears. They knew they had witnessed something special.
CWU coach Gary Frederick called it simply "unbelievable."

It would seem unbelievable to many if this were to happen in
the church today—if those who have been fighting and compet-
ing with one another would begin to run together, to carry the
wounded. We'd hear the cheers and see the tears of those who
would be amazed, moved, and changed by what they've never
seen before: the church acting like the Church.

But it's not unbelievable. Because God believes in you. He
has carried you many times, hasn't he? And if you have not yet
believed in him, I hope that you soon will. Because then you,
too, will know what it is to be carried by him.

The game is not over. We can still reach home safely. That's
what we *will* do, I pray. One thing I know for sure. That's what
we would do . . .

If God were real.

Notes

Introduction

1. David Aikman, *The Delusion of Disbelief* (Carol Stream, Ill.: Tyndale, 2008), 2.
2. Sam Harris, *Letter to a Christian Nation* (New York: Knopf, 2006), 3–4.
3. Lauren Sandler, *Righteous: Dispatches from the Evangelical Youth Movement* (New York: Viking, 2006), 4.
4. Ibid., 10–11.
5. Ibid., 11.
6. Ibid., 247.
7. Ibid.
8. Shane Claiborne, *The Irresistible Revolution* (Grand Rapids: Zondervan, 2006), 72.
9. Harris, *Letter to a Christian Nation,* 5.

1: If God Were Real . . . the Illusions of Ordinary Life Would Be Shattered

1. Gary Witherall with Elizabeth Cody Newenhuyse, *Total Abandon* (Wheaton, Ill.: Tyndale, 2005).
2. Søren Kierkegaard, *Provocations: Spiritual Writings of Kierkegaard,* comp. Charles E. Moore (Farmington, Penn: Broderhof Foundation, 2002), 201.
3. www.newnational.com/joy/joy.html
4. www.newnational.com/joy/isisnt.html
5. See note 4.
6. Ibid.

7. Penn Jillette, interview with Glenn Beck, CNN, November 7, 2007.

8. Penn Jillette, essay, "There Is No God," on *Morning Edition,* NPR, November 21, 2005.

2: If God Were Real . . .
We'd All Give Up on Christianity

1. Charles Colson and Harold Fickett, *The Faith* (Grand Rapids: Zondervan, 2008), 28.

2. Hemant Mehta, *I Sold My Soul on eBay* (Colorado Springs: WaterBrook, 2007), 4.

3. Reggie McNeal, *The Present Future* (San Francisco: Jossey-Bass, 2003), 142.

4. Mehta, *I Sold My Soul on eBay,* 6.

5. Sandler, *Righteous,* 91.

6. Ibid.

7. Claiborne, *Irresistible Revolution,* 117.

8. Nancy Gibbs, "J. K. Rowling," *Time,* December 17, 2007.

9. Ibid.

10. Ibid.

11. Ibid.

12. Ibid.

13. A. W. Tozer, *That Incredible Christian* (Harrisburg, Penn.: Christian Publications, 1964), 71.

14. Gibbs, "J. K. Rowling."

15. Ibid.

16. Ibid.

17. Michael Frost and Alan Hirsch, *The Shaping of Things to Come* (Peabody, Mass.: Hendrickson, 2003), 5.

3: If God Were Real . . .
Missionaries Would Lose Their Jobs

1. McNeal, *Present Future,* 15.

2. Ibid., 141.
3. Jim Cymbala, *Fresh Wind, Fresh Fire* (Grand Rapids: Zondervan, 1997), 53.
4. Ibid., 58–59.
5. McNeal, *Present Future,* 145.

4: If God Were Real . . . Our Family Life
Would Shock the World

1. David Kinnaman and Gabe Lyons, *unChristian* (Grand Rapids: Baker, 2007), 139.
2. Lisa Simpson in "Bart Gets an F," *The Simpsons,* The Simpsons Archive, www.snpp.com/episodes/7F03.html (accessed September 22, 2008).
3. Bart Simpson in "The Joy of Sect," *The Simpsons,* The Simpsons Archive, www.snpp.com/episodes/5F23 (accessed September 22, 2008).
4. Homer Simpson in "Bart vs. Thanksgiving," *The Simpsons,* The Simpsons Archive, www.snpp.com/episodes/7F07.html (accessed September 22, 2008).
5. Richard Dawkins, quoted in "The Church of the Non-Believers," by Gary Wolf, *Wired* magazine, Issue 14.11, November 2006. Available at http://www.wired.com/wired/archive/14.11/atheism.html?pg=2.
6. Dinesh D'Souza, *What's So Great About Christianity?* (Washington, D.C.: Regnery, 2007), 35.
7. Mark Batterson, *In a Pit with a Lion on a Snowy Day* (Colorado Springs: Multnomah, 2006), 56.

5: If God Were Real . . . The Church
Would Be Full of Addicts

1. Nelson Price, quote 135 in *Draper's Book of Quotations for the Christian World* (Wheaton, Ill.: Tyndale, 1992), 139.
2. *The New York Times,* March 12, 2008.

3. A. W. Tozer, *The Pursuit of God, The Pursuit of Man* (Camp Hill, Penn.: Christian Publications, 2002), 6.
4. Quoted in Tozer, *Pursuit of God, Pursuit of Man*, 8.

6: If God Were Real . . .
We'd Live in a Messed-up World

1. Timothy Keller, *The Reason for God: Belief in an Age of Skepticism* (New York: Dutton, 2008), 156.
2. Ibid., 170.
3. Joel Belz, "Practical Atheism," *World* magazine, December 8, 2007, 4.
4. Keller, *Reason for God*, 170.
5. Robert Ferrigno, *Sins of the Assassin* (New York: Scribner, 2008), 163.
6. Eric Swanson, "To Transform a City," Externally Focused Network, www.externallyfocusednetwork.com/free_downloads/transform_a_city.pdf (accessed September 23, 2008), 22.
7. Robert C. Linthicum, *City of God, City of Satan* (Grand Rapids: Zondervan, 1991), 105.

7: If God Were Real . . . You Would
Be Really, Really Rich

1. Kinnaman and Lyons, *unChristian*, 123.
2. Douglas Preston, *Blasphemy* (New York: Forge, 2008, ©2007), 184.
3. Sandler, *Righteous*, 244.
4. Ibid., 247.

8: If God Were Real . . . He Would Believe in Atheists

1. Preston, *Blasphemy*, 146–148.
2. Aikman, *Delusion of Disbelief*, 91.
3. Sandler, *Righteous*, 234.

9: If God Were Real . . . He'd Send Revival!

1. George Barna, *Revolution* (Wheaton, Ill.: Tyndale, 2005), 38.

2. Jim Wallis, *The Great Awakening* (New York: HarperCollins, 2008), 2.

3. *New York Times* editorial, March 20, 1858, quoted in "The Great Awakening of 1857–1858," The Knoxville Revival, www.knoxvillerevival.com/Revivals/greatawakening18572.htm (accessed September 23, 2008).

4. Quoted in *Handbook of Revivals* by Henry C. Fish (Boston: James H. Earle, 1874), 77–78.

5. Barna, *Revolution,* 8.

6. Wallis, *Great Awakening,* 15.

THE
Author, Book & Conversation

JOHN AVANT

I know God is real, because He takes care of crazy people like me:

- I feed sharks with no cage and bring my son. (My wife says if they eat Trey, just stay down there!)

- I may be the only preacher still alive to pick up a green mamba in Africa. (Long story, but I thought it was a grass snake.)

- I dive in underwater caves in Mexico where the Mayans sacrificed humans. (Seriously, this is cool!)

- I like to hang out in the Middle East. (Some of the best people and the best food in the world are there!)

- I de-stress by climbing twenty feet up a tree with a stick and a string and sit there completely still for hours. (If you know what this means, you will rejoice with me that I have my first Pope and Young!)

- To keep from being a fat preacher, I run—a lot. In the Atlanta half-marathon, I was once passed by a woman. Pushing her baby in a stroller! (I sucked it up and passed her at the finish line for one of my great sports achievements.)

- If they had ADD when I was a kid, I would have been the dictionary definition. Even now, I like to work out by running on a treadmill while watching TV, listening to my iPod, and reading from my kindle. (That's not quite enough multitasking for me, but there's no more room for anything else on the treadmill.)

- For fun, I took my son bear hunting with a bow and arrow, sitting behind a bush fifteen yards away. (He shot a monster. I got a new pair of pants.)

- I have dragged my wife to deserts and jungles, mountains and villages, and to some of the real hellholes of this world—just for the awesome privilege of seeing a little heaven born there. (And not only has she stayed around—I think she likes it!)

What was the creative spark that motivated you to write this book?

I spent a few years at a mission agency where I was in churches all across North America. I began to be really concerned that I just didn't see a lot of evidence that most Christians and churches actually believed in God—at least not the God we have said we believed in. It just seemed to me that we had become so different from the first followers of Jesus, it was hard to argue we actually *were* His followers. My friendships with atheists and other nonbelievers confirmed that they didn't see much in us that drew them to faith. But New Testament faith was contagious! I began to yearn to live like God is real—and to find fellow travelers to journey with.

What is the key thought you want readers to take away from this book?

I want nonbelievers to take a fresh look at the possibility of God in a non-threatening way. I hope that Jesus followers will revolt against what we have called Christianity and instead pursue the awesome, passionate, scary-but-worth-it-all journey of living like God is really real.

Why did you choose to approach this topic, even though it may be somewhat controversial?

The church is worth it. Unlike some, I haven't given up on the church. I just don't think we have tried it yet! Most of our churches look so different from the biblical picture of the church, it is hard to make a case that they are churches at all. I love the churches I have served. I want my grandchildren to experience the vibrancy of a community of Jesus followers. If a lot of us don't raise the alarm right now, we are going down the same deadly road as the church in Western Europe. So maybe what I write about is controversial. But it won't be for long. Either we will change and live like God is real, or there won't be enough of us left in a generation or so to have a good controversy!

So are you optimistic or pessimistic about the future of the Church?

Oh, I am an optimist! There are signs all around us of churches of many different styles and sizes who are beginning to live like God is real—and are having a blast! They are following Jesus into the real needs of lives and communities. They are not content just to show up on Sunday and get "charged up" to make it through the next week. They believe the mission of the early church is still theirs—to join Jesus in the advance of the Kingdom and the transformation of whole cities. What a kick it is to be a part of that! I believe these kinds of churches will stand the test of time and will send seeds into the wind that will bear fruit everywhere. Just read someone like Francis Chan and try to be pessimistic about the future! I am a huge optimist about the church that lives like God is real. I am a complete pessimist about religious clubs that pass themselves off as churches.

What's the most important thing the church has to do right now to begin living like God is real?

I asked that question of Billy Graham in December. I had the privilege of visiting with him in his home. His answer was very short and very simple: "Tell the people to pray." Dr. Graham said that prayer was the whole secret of his life and he didn't think Christians really understood its power at all. Think about it—how would we pray if we believed God were real? We'd have to sell tickets to our prayer meetings, wouldn't we? To have a personal meeting with the Creator of the universe where He unleashes His power? I want to share life with Jesus followers who want to really live this way!

1. Meditate on this for a moment: What evidence would nonbelievers see in your life that suggest you truly believe that God is real?

2. Ask someone to honestly evaluate your life: What about you indicates that you believe God is real? What about you could cause someone to doubt that you really believe God is real?

3. What would happen in your community if your church vanished from the earth today? Does your church live like God is real, making such an impact in the community that they could not carry on without you?

4. Are you really willing to change your own life and your church in order to live like God is real? What if that change was uncomfortable? What if you didn't like the music or preaching anymore? Are you really interested in following Jesus—or just enjoying church?

5. How does your family life impact others? Do you isolate your family from nonbelievers, or do you pursue relationships with those who are different from you like Jesus did? What makes this so hard to do, and what can you do to make changes?

6. Define a Christian. How does that word change when you add "ity" to it? How would you say the Christianity you see around you is like the movement Jesus founded? How is it different? What can you do about it?

7. How many nonbelievers do you know well? When is the last time you had dinner with a nonbeliever, had a nonbeliever to your house or went to theirs like Jesus did with Zacchaeus or Matthew? What makes that so hard, and how can you overcome it?

8. How do you join Jesus in His pursuit of the "lost sheep" without living like you are lost yourself? What safeguards do you need when really engaging nonbelievers?

9. What does it mean to you to live a missioner's life? Would you say your life is defined by mission? Or is mission just a part of your life? Is your church defined by its mission? What is the evidence of that? How could you change to live a truly missioner life?

10. Have you or your church been involved in disputes and controversies? What have they been about? Fulfilling the Great Commission? Giving yourselves away for the sake of the cross? If they have been about lesser things, what will you do to avoid being distracted in the future from living as if God is real?

11. How do you pray? Does your prayer life indicate that you actually believe God is real? What are your church prayer meetings like? How are they attended? Do you see evidence that your church believes that if you will meet together to pray, the real God will move in transformational power? If not, how would you begin to change?

12. Are there things in your life that you crave more than God? Is that evidence that you may be living as if God is not real? How can your church help those who are struggling with addictions that serve as replacement idols for the real God?

13. What does it mean to you to take eternity seriously? Do you evaluate the real wealth of your life by the measures of this world or the next?

14. What might a movement of God look like in your community? How could you be a part of it? What is the one thing you most need to change to live like God is real and be ready to be used by Him? What is the one thing your church most needs to change?